"A book as wise and warm-hearted as talking to a good friend over a cup of tea. "

—MUSHIM (PATRICIA) IKEDA, Buddhist teacher
and writer

"A warm, perceptive, and helpful exploration of Buddhist truths by a Zen priest who brings her awareness of difference and the suffering it causes to her practice of this ancient spiritual path. Earthlyn asks us to step up to our lives and be present for them, to offer compassion to ourselves and others, to expand our vision to allow for a spacious, tender engagement with our precious days and hours."

—SANDY BOUCHER, author of *Turning the Wheel: American Women Creating the New Buddhism*

"Zenju Earthlyn Manuel's book is a lyrically written description of how the teachings of the Buddha are relevant to all communities in our contemporary world. Her words are simple and yet penetrating, covering philosophy, technique, and the ineffable qualities of experiencing a spiritual life."

—LARRY YANG, Buddhist teacher

"Thank you, Earthlyn, for presenting such a personally moving, beautiful and artistic book. Your testimony reveals both the diversity and humanity of the Buddha's teachings. This publication is an inspiration calling for many of us to dare such an authentic tasting and expression of the benefits of the Buddhist path."

—LARRY WARD, Dharma teacher, practitioner

Lindiña
te Quiero
mucho!
tu Amiga,
Susan

Praise for
TELL ME SOMETHING ABOUT BUDDHISM

"*Tell Me Something about Buddhism* is a dharma gem of great wisdom. Just reading Zenju Earthlyn Manuel's clear, beautiful, and inspiring answers to questions about Buddhist practice quieted and calmed my mind as quickly as the wood striking wood sound of a *han* calling me to awakening."

—CHARLES JOHNSON, author of *Turning the Wheel:
Essay on Buddhism and Writing* and *Middle Passage*,
winner of the National Book Award

"In homage to her ancestors, Zenju Earthlyn Manuel shares a very personal journey with many gems of wisdom to help heal the sufferings of racism and other human afflictions. What does it mean to be black and Buddhist?"

—KARMA LESKHE TSOMO, SR. Tibetan Nun,
founder of Sakyadhita.org

"Drawing on her many years of practice, Zenju Earthlyn Manuel has brought her lived experience to her lucid and compassionate responses to many questions often asked by newcomers to Buddhism. This book is also a heartfelt response to her younger sister's question, 'What does Buddhism have to do with black people?' She says, 'I knew, in the moment my sister asked the question, that the Buddha's teachings had everything to do with me and with every other suffering living being.'

—SENSEI ZENKEI BLANCHE HARTMAN, Sr. Dharma
Teacher at the San Francisco Zen Center

"I have read many books on Buddhism in the last twenty five years but this one heralds the arrival of a bracingly fresh, talented new teacher. Manuel's ability to distill the teachings and describe in personal, honest terms her own engagement with them makes for a read that is lucid and affecting, unassuming yet universal. Her words land on you as if spoken to you and your situation alone. Her disarming style gives you a sense of inclusion, confidence and empowerment in the prospect of connecting with your own light and wisdom yet she never loses sight of the complicated, often painful realities of our society. Her arrival represents a whole 'turning of the wheel' of Buddhism taking root on Western soil."

—CANYON SAM, author of *Sky Train: Tibetan Women on the Edge of History*, winner of PEN American Center Award

"I appreciate the clear and direct way that Zenju's introduction to Buddhism points to both the North Star and the moon. Those of us who followed the North Star sense that the path of liberation is endless. Of all those who encounter her offering, I especially hope her book reaches those whose cultural legacy has been the longing for freedom."

—SENSEI MERLE KYODO BOYD, Zen priest, Dharma teacher at Zen Center of Los Angeles

"Zenju Earthlyn Manuel's book *Tell Me Something about Buddhism* offers both the story of her spiritual rite of passage from a black girl to a Buddhist priest and a hands-on manual with the basic questions that many are afraid to ask."

—DR. MARLENE JONES, contributor, *Dharma, Color, and Culture: New Voices in Western Buddhism*

"Discover and enjoy the freedom that's your birthright. Zenju Earthlyn Manuel asks the important questions… and brings home the answers. This simple book makes the Buddha's timeless teachings real, for all, for here and now. Ordinary life is precious life. I'm grateful for her guidance along the Path."

— GARY GACH, author of *The Complete Idiot's Guide to Buddhism* and editor of *What Book!?: Buddha Poems from Beat to Hip Hop*

"With the effort and application that can only come through disciplined spiritual practice, Zenju Earthlyn Manuel's *Tell Me Something about Buddhism* is written with the practical clear-sightedness of the highly polished mirror of transcendence."

— CLAUDE ANSHIN THOMAS, Vietnam veteran & Zen Buddhist monk, author of the award-winning *At Hell's Gate: A Soldier's Journey from War to Peace*

TELL ME SOMETHING ABOUT
BUDDHISM

questions and answers for the curious beginner

ZENJU EARTHLYN MANUEL

HAMPTON ROADS

Cover design by Jim Warner
Cover art © Zenju Earthlyn Manuel
Illustrations by Zenju Earthlyn Manuel
Book Design by Maureen Forys, Happenstance Type-O-Rama

Hampton Roads Publishing Company, Inc.
Charlottesville, VA 22906
www.redwheelweiser.com

Quotations of gathas (page 30) from *Happiness: Essential Mindfulness Practices* (2009) by Thich Nhat Hanh, are reprinted with permission of Parallax Press, Berkeley, California, (www.parallax.org).

"Fire of Transformation" (page 35) © Mark Nepo, reprinted with his permission (www.marknepo.com).

"Seas" by Juan Ramón Jiménez (page 45) reprinted by permission from *The Poet and the Sea* (Buffalo, NY: White Pine Press, 2009), translated by Mary Berg and Dennis Maloney.

"Case One" (page 105), from the *Book of Serenity: One Hundred Zen Dialogues*, translated by Thomas Cleary (licensed to Shambhala, 2005), reprinted by permission from Steiner Books.

Library of Congress Cataloging-in-Publication Data available upon request

ISBN: 978-1-57174-658-0

Printed in the United States of America
MAL
10 9 8 7 6 5 4 3 2 1

Homage to Shakyamuni Buddha

Homage to Mahapajapati, Great Mother

Homage to Kuan Yin, Bodhisattva of compassion

Homage to all the native tribes of the land I was born

Homage to all the ancestors that have led me to the path

般若波羅蜜多心經

觀自在菩薩行深般
若波羅蜜多時照見
五蘊皆空度一切苦厄。
舍利子色不異空空
不異色色即是空空
即是色受想行識亦
復如是舍利子是諸
法空相不生不滅不
垢不淨不增不減是
故空中無色無受想行識
無色

DEDICATION TO THE ANCESTORS

I touch the earth. I honor you ancestors with my sitting meditation practice. I do so as an extension of our lives. I see you. I am born each moment with you. I walk with you. I heal with you. Let each breath be a gift of my love.

My given name is Earthlyn Marselean Manuel. My dharma name is Ekai Zenju.

I am one of three daughters born to Alvesta Pierre Manuel and Lawrence Manuel, Jr.

I am the granddaughter of Emma Louise Broussard Pierre and Theodore Pierre, Marceline Henderson and Lawrence Manuel, Sr.

I am the great granddaughter of Madeline Baysan Broussard and Josiah Broussard.

I am a great, great granddaughter of Africa and of many other continents on earth.

I bow to each and every ancestor.

Invite the Bell

CONTENTS

FOREWORD

Buddhism is like a tree that is constantly growing and adapting to the new lands and cultures it is brought to. For the Buddha's teachings to stay healthy and vibrant, we must constantly renew and update them so they remain relevant and effective for the increasingly diverse communities that practice them. Zen underlines the importance of skillfulness in bringing students to a deeper understanding of awakening. In this book, with its engaging and accessible question-and-answer format, Zenju Earthlyn brings the Buddha's teachings alive in a fresh and powerful voice born from her own fully lived experience of transformation.

Zenju Earthlyn helps us all to realize that the past and future are here in the present moment. The secret of transformation is in the way we take care of this very moment. To promote the work of transformation, we should practice with a Sangha, a community in which everyone has the intention to learn and practice. But good intentions are not enough. We need to learn the art of forming a harmonious community which can give people a feeling of confidence.

In her humble, authentic, and down-to-earth style, Zenju Earthlyn is a true spiritual friend, a generous and fearless agent of Dr. Martin Luther King, Jr.'s Beloved Community, helping to build the Beloved Sangha by opening her arms and heart wide for many people to touch the healing wisdom of the Buddha. We can all practice like her, as cells in the larger body of our communities, helping others touch peace through our own practice of understanding and compassion.

—THICH NHAT HANH
  Plum Village, France, 2011

INTRODUCTION

WHAT IS BUDDHISM?

I hope you are well today. As I continue to follow the path, I encounter many people who have never been introduced to the teachings of Buddha and who become curious about Buddhist practice. There is even more curiosity when they see that my skin is black and that I clearly have African ancestry. Many have asked, "How did you come to an ancient Asian practice, such as Buddhism, as an African American person?"

First, it is important to say there is no country called Asia and that the terms *Asia* and *Asian* encompass many Eastern countries and many diverse people from those countries. That being said, I can clearly say that Buddha's teachings came from the ancient dirt of India all the way to my doorstep in contemporary California USA. Specifically, what brought me to the path of Buddha is the same thing that brings many folks to any spiritual practice: suffering and needing a place to heal.

On the other hand, I did not choose Buddha's path as much as I had been chosen by it. At first, I didn't see myself as practicing Buddhism or anything else from India, China, or Japan. To say out loud that I was practicing Buddhism felt like separating myself from my Christian upbringing and from other black people. In the beginning, I just had this secret: I was doing something different.

I didn't go out of the way to find Buddha's path. His teachings met me at the door of my own suffering. And when they came knocking over twenty years ago, I actually ran the other way. I was afraid of something so new and different from the black church I was raised in or the Yoruba African religion that I had been called to in my younger days. I told the Buddhist teachers that I did not have any room in my life for chanting, sitting down after work, or altars that were Japanese.

Still, the teachers didn't go away, bringing me candles, special Japanese incense that I had never seen before, and books to read. I had met my match. They were more stubborn than I could ever imagine. But it wasn't their persistence that kept me still long enough to invite the teachings in. I never sent the teachers away because I recognized the innate kindness and compassion in the words of Buddha that they shared. I recognized the teachings about compassion and wisdom as something I had been yearning to hear. I was dying inside, so to speak, and found vitality in chanting and meditation. Then I heard the voice of God, the love that God represents, in the teachings of Buddha. I was hooked.

Once, my youngest sister asked, "What does Buddhism have to do with black people?"

Although Shakyamuni Buddha's teachings came from the earth of ancient India, I knew, in the moment my sister asked the question, that the teachings had everything to do with me and with every other suffering living being. Of course, she wanted to know how did I come to such a strange journey, when she knew me as a devout Christian, a courageous warrior of the black civil rights movement, and a dedicated Pan-Africanist. She knew me with my Afro hairdo, African headwraps, and African jewelry. She knew the sister who read aloud poetry by black poets such as Langston Hughes, Nikki Giovanni, the Last Poets, Margaret Walker, and Gwendolyn Brooks. I was speaking to her through the words of the poets about our experiences as young black women.

Later, after living with her question a bit longer, I began to see that the answer was as large as an elephant and that I had touched only its tail when I attempted to answer my sister's profound question with, "Because it works." I believe my sister's question was about her need to heal from not having been universally loved as a dark-skinned, loving woman. She knew that her question was an inquiry about my own life. She needed to know how would I help black people by being a Zen Buddhist priest. In the moment she asked, I couldn't find a way to convey to her that much of what I experienced in being black was much like what the Buddha taught.

I understood his teachings because I was raised with poor people, much like the ones Buddha saw when he left the temple. I was taught generosity without the notion of gain because it was not expected that everyone *could* give in return. I was taught compassion for having slave ancestry. I held a sense of spiritual equanimity while experiencing discrimination. My family and those around us lived with a communal sense in which everyone and everything was related—something that is called interbeing in the mindfulness community. Generosity, compassion, equanimity, and interbeingness were all essential to our survival. It was the way we embodied harmony. Buddha's message to me was about healing and regaining a sense of belonging within the community of living beings into which I was born. Being on the path of Buddha was a way of experiencing, as Charles Johnson, an African American Buddhist teacher and author puts it, "a long-deferred peace." To follow the ancient teachings of Buddha was to be life affirming. On the path of Buddha's teachings, I returned, through chanting and meditation, to that place within that had not been touched by the suffering of hatred. In following the path of Buddha, I began to peel off the masks that covered my original face. In the practice of Buddha's love, I eventually became aware of my life in all of its difficult and glorious moments.

In the end, I know the teachings of Buddha go beyond Buddha, beyond the shape of things as they appear. There is no way to point to Buddhism and say, "There it is." Yet I find myself cuddling up to a *sense* of it just when the roar of life seems too loud.

For these reasons, I decided to offer this book to those who want to learn something about Buddhism. By no means have I covered the vastness of Buddha's teachings here. A myriad of books by numerous teachers, both Eastern and Western, offer a more thorough explanation of the teachings. It is important to say here that I am at the beginning of my journey as Zen priest, and I am referred to as a novice in our lineage. Therefore, what I share in this book derives from my direct experience of the practice as a student and as a dharma sister for more than twenty years. With the assistance of several dharma-transmitted Zen teachers, I created this offering to help clarify some aspects of Buddhism.

First, I would like to say that Buddha's teachings are similar to all other ancient teachings. His core teachings were much like those of Jesus, Mohammed, Sojourner Truth, White Buffalo Woman (who brought the *Chanupa*, or sacred pipe, to the Lakota), many unnamed indigenous medicine people, and other sages of old. They are similar in the sense that they address our connection to each other and ways to mend that connection when we cannot remember the relationship of all things.

Many ask, "What is Buddhism?" before they ask, "Who is Buddha?" The word *Buddhism* is only a name conjured up—centuries after Buddha's life—to capture all that Buddha taught. So though people ask, "What is Buddhism?" they might get a more accurate response if they asked, "Who was Buddha and what did Buddha teach?"

QUESTIONS AND ANSWERS

⚅ Who was Buddha and what did he teach?

The word *Buddha* is Sanskrit meaning "the awakened one," a person who has been released from the world of cyclic existence *(samsara)* and attained liberation from desire. A Buddha realizes that desire is an indication of one's dissatisfaction. Recognizing dissatisfaction can become an open gate to the path of liberation. Buddha experienced such dissatisfaction with life before he began his quest for enlightenment.

There were many who carried the name *Buddha* before the one popular Buddha was born. Shakyamuni Buddha, born Siddartha Gautama in Kapilavatsu, India, was the one popular Buddha we speak of today. He was born into the Shakyan tribe and thus given the name Shakyamuni Buddha, meaning "the awakened one of the Shakyan tribe." His father was King Suddhodana. His mother, Mayadevi, known as the Great Mother, died seven days after his birth, so his aunt Mahapajapati raised him. He lived as a wealthy, protected prince, married a woman of royalty named Yasodhara, and had a son, named Rahula.

Once he became aware of all the suffering that had been hidden from him, including old age, sickness, birth, and death, he left his family's palace. He went to many teachers to understand this suffering, and they taught him various lessons about ending suffering. He excelled with all of his teachers, to the point that they asked him to become a teacher. However, Buddha refused their invitations to teach, feeling he had not yet been fully awakened to the condition of suffering. He continued his journey.

Fortunately, Buddha was a dreamer. His first teachings came from a succession of five dreams. Finally, after sitting among the trees in the forest, he became a lamp unto himself and was enlightened to what he called the Four Noble Truths of Suffering. These truths are:

1. There is suffering.

2. There is a cause for suffering.

3. There is cessation of suffering.

4. There is a path leading to the end of suffering, called the Eightfold Path.

🕉 Can you tell me more about the Four Noble Truths of Suffering?

There is suffering (*dukkha*). *Dukkha* means suffering. This first truth brings awareness to the universal law that we all suffer in some way. Physical suffering is called *dukkha dukkha*, when there is pain or disease in the body. Mental and emotional suffering is called *samsara dukkha*, in which there is dissatisfaction or anguish or a thirst for pleasure, power, and prosperity. Also, this kind of suffering includes seeing one's individual existence or having notions of being separate from all things and being. Spiritual suffering is called *viparinama dukkha*, which is resisting change, not understanding that all things are impermanent.

There is a cause for suffering (*samudaya*). *Samudaya* means the arising of suffering. This second truth addresses the origin, roots, nature, or creation of suffering. We are invited as practitioners to explore our suffering so that we can touch the root of it. The root can take on the nature of clinging to desires, ideas, expectations, and attachment to who we think we are in this lifetime.

There is cessation of suffering (*nirodha*). *Nirodha* means "cessation," to end suffering. After becoming aware of the root of suffering, we are encouraged in the practice to cease an engagement with the things that cause suffering. More specifically, we are taught to be aware of our actions through body, mind, and speech.

There is a path leading to the end of suffering (*magga*). *Magga* means "path," and in this case, it is the path of awakening. There is a path out of suffering, a path that can shift our tendency from suffering toward liberation. It is commonly called the Noble Eightfold Path. The path includes Right View or understanding, Right Intention, Right Speech, Right Action, Right Livelihood, Right Effort, Right Mindfulness, and Right Concentration.

The word *right* has been used as a translation of the Pali word *samma*, which appears in Buddha's original sermon (or *sutras*, meaning "teachings," as they are commonly called). *Samma* has also been translated to mean "perfect" or "complete." However, it literally stands for the quietude of *citta*, or mind upon itself. The entire path is *samma*; every aspect of the path has *samma*. One's whole life is *samma*. The complete or perfect knowing of the whole series of each moment of our lives is *damma*. Therefore, for the sake of avoiding a sense of right and wrong or confusing this path with rules, I prefer to use the word *complete* in the place of *right*. *Complete* refers to doing what is beneficial to living an awakened life, living in a way that does not cause suffering. The path aligns with actions of the body, speech, and heart-mind.

The ancient Eightfold Path espoused by Shakyamuni Buddha invites us to take a vow to awaken to life as we are living it or to awaken to suffering. It is a vow so expansive it includes awakening to not only our own suffering, but also the suffering of others. It is a vow that is not meant to be an achievement we boast about with our friends, but an inexhaustible commitment to embrace the path, despite our being weary.

Walking the Eightfold Path is a vow to break through things that have obstructed our liberation such as the constant yearning for pleasure, power, and prosperity. It is a path that has to do with being vigilant *and* one in which the fragility, vulnerability, and soft centers of our hearts are revealed in the transformation and evolution of life.

Yet this path cannot be taught, as it is wisdom that must surface within. You can only bring it alive with the actions of your life. You cannot just memorize it or find techniques of liberated speaking and behaving. The path can only be engaged by your living of it. It can only be engaged as an awakening of your own doing. The path is difficult to grasp because it goes against our instincts to intellectually figure it out first rather than living it. We might say,

"I don't want to do this until I know what it is." We might say, "Prove that this will work when all else has failed." We are stymied by our instinct to doubt its legitimacy. For these reasons, there exist practices such as meditation and sacred time, like vision quests, to help pry open the closed doors of our lives.

At first glance, the teachings on the Four Noble Truths appear simple, but to understand how suffering arises and ceases can take a lifetime. For further reading on these teachings, I suggest *The Heart of the Buddha's Teachings* by the renowned Vietnamese Zen teacher Thich Nhat Hanh.

⌘ Would you say Buddha experienced a vision quest?

I like to say Buddha experienced a vision quest when he went into the world to seek answers to his questions on suffering. Also, I like to say Buddha met his ancestors in his five dreams and received teachings. But followers of Buddha would not speak of his journey in terms of a vision quest. And rarely do we hear about Buddha's teachings emerging through lucid dreams.

Imagine Buddha committing himself to sitting among a forest of trees. Imagine spiritual teachers training him to see beyond the physical realms of life. These teachers taught him how to live on little food in the forest, how to survive the harsh climate with very little clothing, and how to attain deep, altered states of consciousness and to surrender to the spirit of nature. Just as shamans in indigenous cultures prepare for a holy life as teachers and healers, Buddha prepared for his initiation, his near-death experience, and his ultimate illumination on the suffering of living beings.

According to his sermons, his quest for understanding centered around these questions: What are these things of suffering I am subject to in life? What were these things of suffering that existed before my birth?

This spiritual curiosity is what moved Buddha to leave home. He did the difficult action of leaving behind his family for a time to enter into a state of meditation in which the sacred mysteries of life would surface from within. He shaved his head and wrapped himself in a saffron-colored cloth to indicate to others that he was taking up a spiritual quest, an odyssey of sorts. Joined by five other monks, he went into the forest, among the trees, and there each one found a place alone where the inner voice would be awakened and the state of the unborn revealed. In the forest he would open to his own suffering, which had been hidden from him all his life.

It was in the wilderness that Buddha would begin to experience lucid dreams and have visions of liberation from suffering. The remote jungle was hard to endure; seclusion was hard to embrace, and isolation was difficult to enjoy. Buddha experienced the same fear as any of us would in such a situation. In his own words, he reveals that he was afraid:

But there are the specially holy nights of the half moons of the fourteenth and fifteenth, and the quarter moon of the eighth; suppose I spent those nights in such awe-inspiring abodes as

*orchard shrines, woodland shrines and tree shrines, which
make the hair stand up—perhaps I should encounter that fear
and dread? And later [on one of those holy nights] . . . a deer
would approach me, or a peacock would knock off a branch
. . . Surely this is the fear and dread coming . . . And while I
walked, the fear and dread came upon me, but I neither stood
nor sat nor lay down till I had subdued the fear and dread.*

Yet Buddha remained in the forest, working to not be
overwhelmed by his fear and dread. He spent time doing
all kinds of things to gain power over his mind. What came
to him was the idea of clenching his teeth and pressing his
tongue against the roof of his mouth to constrain his mind.
It was recorded that he said, "Sweat ran from my armpits
while I did so." Then he decided to practice meditation without breathing. And when he did this, he is recorded saying, "Violent winds racked my head, as if a strong man were
splitting my head open with a sharp sword."

He had exhausted himself with painful efforts to gain
power over his mind when he decided one final renunciation—to cut off food or have very little food. And he made
this decision after having been in the forest for quite some
time. Finally, he reached an extreme emaciated state. He
said, "My limbs became like the jointed segments of vine
stems or bamboo stems, because of eating so little. My
backside became like a camel's hoof; the projections on my
spine stood forth like corded beads, my ribs jutted out as
gaunt as the crazy rafters of an old roofless barn . . . If
I touched my belly skin, I encountered my backbone too.

8

If I tried to ease my body by rubbing my limbs with my hands, the hair, rotted at its roots, fell away from my body as I rubbed."

Soon after this near-death experience from not eating enough food, Buddha realized austerity was not the way to enlightenment. To be enlightened, he needed his body because it was his body, his life, from which awakening would occur. He was offered milk from a young girl who saw him, and soon after he began to eat solid food.

Upon Buddha's release of austere approaches and techniques of gaining *power over* his mind, he allowed his mind to settle upon itself in a quiet way. It was then that the teachings of the earth surfaced through his bones. Five dreams appeared to him as he continued his practice of deep, meditative absorption.

First he dreamed that the great earth was his couch, the Himalayan Mountains his pillow. His left hand lay in the eastern ocean, his right hand lay in the western ocean, and his feet lay in the southern ocean. This dream informed him of full enlightenment to come.

In the second dream, a creeping animal (presumed to be a snake) grew up out of his navel and stood touching the clouds. There are statues of Buddha with a snake climbing his body that represents this dream. This second dream, in particular, was said to be a premonition of the Four Noble Truths. He would come to call the emergence of these initial teachings *Turning the Wheel of Dharma*, symbolizing a circular path to liberation from suffering. It was the second dream that would give rise to his shamanic voice.

His third dream of four birds of different colors turning white foretold that he would have followers on his path, dressed in white, who would take refuge in his teachings. In some Buddhist traditions, white is worn by followers in the initial steps toward full ordination.

His fourth dream revealed that when his teachings were heard, the four castes—the warrior-nobles, the Brahmin priests, the burgesses, and the plebians (possibly like the Dalits today)—would see his teachings as truth and be delivered from the caste system. Yet still today, many have not heard his teachings, and if they have, they have refused to accept them as truth.

His fifth dream warned him of greed or delusion in regard to the gifts that would be bestowed upon him, such as food, housing, medicine, and robes. Only Buddha would know of his own greed and delusion. However, in modern times, this dream can serve as a warning to all who receive gifts for their teachings.

In the end, Buddha was a man with all the frailties of any human being. He answered a call to sit in the woods and watch his own past dissolve. He saw his own death, and his death became a twilight filled with teachings.

At the end of seven days, Buddha rose from his concentration at the root of the Bodhi Tree, enlightened to the nature of suffering. He then moved from the root of the Bodhi Tree to the root of the Ajapala Nigrodha Tree, and finally to the root of the Banyan Tree.

The sacrifice of nearly dying brought forth in Buddha an awakening to the idea that our bodies and the heart-minds that guide them can bring us into relationship with all living beings (including the earth). If we are not aligned with nature, it can separate us, destroying the fabric that holds us together. When we lose the importance of our relationships, we suffer, and society suffers. Our deepest wisdom is also lost. We grow hungry for ourselves as peacemakers.

⧉ Can we be enlightened?

Fortunately, in revealing the Four Noble Truths, Buddha's own enlightenment became ours. We can all enter the vast state of awakened consciousness. The wisdom we all have is in our own experience of initiation and transformation.

The initiation into enlightenment begins with our own willingness to not only speak of our suffering, but also to understand it as a condition we share as living beings. In my practice, I learned how suffering emerged when I clung to suffering as my personal story when others are involved in the same painful circumstances. I began to ask questions, as Buddha did on his quest. Then I left my palace of the comfort zone, the familiar, and dared myself to go into unknown territory. I wrote:

> She walks through the gate,
> Heavy footed,
> Gazing out from the darkness of skin,
> Seeing no church pews,
> She sits chanting,
> Why have I come without knowing whose house I have entered?

Once I found my place in the world of chanting and sitting meditation, I allowed my body to settle on suffering of any kind—not reenergizing the suffering, but settling on it long enough to turn the stone into soft earth. After some time, I began to feel myself as expansive as the earth, and I acknowledged suffering as part of my life, no longer recoiling from it. In this acknowledgment, I was not on a quest to gain a vision, but on a quest in which a vision of my life might arise on its own. With the acknowledgment of suffering and the practice of complete connection of all things comes enlightenment.

A mental or theoretical investigation of enlightenment will lead directly to confusion. Enlightenment arises without you knowing. You ask, "How will I know?" That is the mystery of this practice. There are no exact formulas that lead to results.

What I will say again is that when Buddha became enlightened, we all became awakened to the truth of suffering. However, our fears and desires hinder us from experiencing such awakening. The practice of chanting and meditation arouses this hidden enlightenment, reminding us of our original nature, which is untouched by suffering. We can chant and meditate through many indigenous traditions, including a myriad of Eastern traditions: Tibetan Buddhism, Shambhala, Zen, Shingon, Jodo Shin, Nichiren, Chinese Ch'an, Theravada, Insight Meditation, T'ai chi, Chi kung (Qigong), vedantic and yogic practices, and so forth. As we journey into these traditions, we can be buddha—that is, we can be awakened. (In our tradition, we use *buddha*—lowercase—to refer to ourselves.)

You can see how the word *Buddhism* is too simple a word for the complexity of Buddha's teachings and approaches to learning and practicing them.

33 Why do Buddhists talk about suffering and not joy?

Many say that Buddhists talk about suffering more than they do about joy or love. This may have some truth, because Buddha's first message to the world was about suffering. He did not say, "If you do this, you will have joy." He simply spoke to the human condition of suffering that he witnessed for himself in the hopes that we would find happiness in understanding suffering. He offered no guarantees or promises about what would happen when one practices these teachings. The joy comes from the individual's dedication to the path and the deepening of one's relationship with other living beings, including four-leggeds, winged ones, trees, plants, and living beings we have yet to meet. For this reason, most Buddhist teachers will not directly say, "If you do this, you will not suffer." They simply sit with you as a spiritual friend in your suffering and share their life experiences in relationship to Buddha's teachings. Teachers sit with students, trusting their interrelationship and shared life experiences with suffering, joy, and love. Eventually, the wisdom that surfaces from within suffering can give rise to liberation from our anguish.

Liberation is joy. It is a joy grounded in dedication and devotion to a path of awakening. There is joy in asking, "How can I be loving to my family, to my friends, to my dharma sisters and brothers?" There is joy in saying, "I am present for you," to all those I love. And we cannot have that joy or love until we understand suffering.

🎴 In your tradition, do you have anything like the Ten Commandments in Christianity or particular ways to treat others?

We are taught to live by what are called precepts or vows. During the ordination ceremony, nuns and monks take these vows, which can number into the hundreds, depending on the tradition. Teachers, family, and friends witness the taking of these vows, so that the ordained is held accountable to all and is aware that he or she has entered into a commitment. However, you do not have to be ordained to follow the precepts.

Before I share some of the precepts, I would like to offer a few words to distinguish the precepts from rules or goals. You can think of precepts as sage wisdom from grandparents or wise elders who have awakened to the nature of life. In many cultures, there are ancient folktales that demonstrate lessons for living in harmony. The precepts are meant to assist us in valuing life and in not judging the self or each other from a righteous place. They are not principles to measure someone's flaws or level of spirituality. There is no external punishment for breaking these precepts. Mostly, the precepts describe how an awakened person lives mindful of the possible suffering caused by his or her actions. In this way of caring for each other, we nurture a spiritually based social justice.

The precepts give you an idea of how one attends to life. In following the precepts, we are conscious of developing a spiritual life. With the precepts, we cultivate, create, and sustain life; give generously; and have sexual relationships that are respectful of the body as life, as a living creation. We offer caring words; we offer timely silence, and we stay aware and awake to how we relate to life.

Yet many of us are afraid. When paralyzed by fear, we cannot value life. Fear keeps us from being aware of anything other than fear. Fear takes away a sense of heart, tenderness, and vulnerability. What are we afraid of?

Maybe we are afraid of rejection, of being harmed, unloved, or not seen for who we "think" we are. But by being afraid of others, we suffer and then become disconnected and ignorant of our interrelationship. We cannot follow the precepts when fear paralyzes our hearts. We lose the ability to transmit light in the world.

In following the precepts, we are transmitters of life light, as Sensei Kobun Chino says:

> *The main subject is how to become a transmitter of actual light, life light. Practice takes place to shape your whole ability to reflect the light coming through you, and to generate and re-generate your system so the light increases its power. Each precept is a remark about hard climbing, maybe climbing down. You don't use the precepts for accomplishing your own personality, or fulfilling your dream of your highest image. You don't use the precepts in that way. The precepts are the reflected light-world of one precept, which is Buddha's mind itself, which is the presence of Buddha.*

(These words from the late Sensei Chino were taken from a handout by Zenkei Blanche Hartman, senior dharma teacher at the San Francisco Zen Center.)

We are all transmitters of light, and yet sometimes our actions can adversely affect an entire group of people. I have experienced this aspect of life many times when I have not remembered to live in harmony with others. The result was suffering for an entire community, much more than I could have ever imagined. If we remember our inherent nature of being connected, we can avoid harming others directly or indirectly. When one is suffering, we are all in the suffering. If someone is acting in such a way as to dishonor life, we are all present for that dishonoring—meaning it is necessary for all to participate in the transformation and healing.

Fortunately, to sustain our light, there is compassion, forgiveness, and reconciliation. There is also the practice of mindfulness to help us follow the precepts and, therefore, value life. With the precepts I will share here, we practice letting go of "you" and "me" and become "us." Bodhidharma, the Indian sage who brought Buddha's teachings to China, taught that to receive the precepts is to realize Buddha Mind or One Mind, the one mind of selflessness—to remember our connection.

These first five precepts are part of what are called the ten grave precepts. They are:

Avoid killing or taking life; instead, cultivate life. Many practice this teaching in an honorable and literal way by not eating meat, not killing insects, or becoming a conscientious objector in the face of war. However, the precept of not killing, in a larger context, can be about imposing death in many ways. When any one of us causes another human being to tremble, we are faced with the prospect of killing another's sense of survival. When we threaten to harm another being or present danger, we are eliminating that being's life force. In this larger view of the teaching, we can kill by engaging in verbal and physical abuse, or denying a living being the basic needs of water, food, clothing and shelter. Having a mind of violence, whether we go through with it or not, does not align with cultivating life. We are to be aware of the many ways in which we may actively take life. We cultivate life when we let go of all weapons—not just the ones created for war, but also the ones used to hurt others, such as gossip, dehumanizing speech, or a refusal to protect life. As beings of the earth, we are to protect life, to protect the oceans, trees, mountains, forests, wildlife, and the air we breathe. We are caretakers who *take care* by cultivating the innate love many of us spend time seeking from other places.

Avoid stealing or taking what isn't given; instead, give generously. Underlining this precept is honesty and reducing the need to accumulate possessions. Taking what is not given can range from taking material items (including money) from someone to exploiting everything and everyone for one's own gain. According to Ngakpa Chogyam Rinpoche, stealing can also take the form of asking too many favors, expecting others to carry you, abusing hospitality, or squandering another's time, energy, and resources. A global example of stealing has occurred during the history of the world when others have robbed groups of people of their land, language, customs, and family for gain.

Instead of stealing, we acknowledge our mind of scarcity. We cease our accumulation of things and people, and learn to offer our gifts. We offer joy, wisdom, and loving ways passed on from generations before us. We act with a loving-grandparent mind, being gentle to our frail sense of survival.

Avoid sexual misconduct; instead, embrace enlightened energy and love. In many spiritual communities in the United States, little is said of sexuality and sex, or what is said often is based in fear and condemnation. In Buddhist communities, this precept can bring a broad discussion of sexuality and sex, but not much is explored afterward.

Of all the levels of unconsciousness, sexual dishonor (or misconduct) is least forgiving in North American culture, for perhaps several reasons. We are sensitized to keep sexual matters secret, we are attached to perfection, and we have superior views of a pure self or hold onto a sense of having not executed or been involved in any sexual dishonor.

Sexual dishonor can include a long list of things, from sending inappropriate computer messages with sexual overtones to lust (private thoughts or open ones), infidelity, to rape, sexual torture, and sexual slavery. Many families have been broken by sexual dishonor, and children have suffered from sexual abuse. I breathe in, and I breathe out to say that it is easy to stumble in this world filled with mixed messages on sex and sexuality. I can say from personal experience it is not easy to continue life under a cloud of sexual dishonor. In healing from such a cloud, I chanted:

I breathe in, and I breathe out, feeling my feet on the ground. Breathing in and breathing out, I let go of those times I could not do any better. Breathing in and breathing out, I am grateful for the help I received. Breathing in and breathing out, I can begin again in the renewal and rejuvenation of the next moment.

Silence about or justification for one's own misconduct, gossip about others' misconduct, ridicule, jokes about the incidents, slander to ruin someone else's reputation, hatred toward the person who is perceived as the perpetrator—all are ways in which any act of sexual dishonor is fueled and perpetuated for years. These actions in response to sexual dishonor also drive the circumstances underground, and the individuals involved as well, out of fear of persecution or being labeled for life. In Buddha's teachings, sexual dishonor is not seen as everlasting simply because of other practices, such as loving-kindness, compassion, forgiveness, and reconciliation. We have little sanctuary for healing these wounds. At the same time, we have the wisdom to know when we are deluded by our own minds. When we can see ourselves, we are awake.

Avoid lying; instead, speak honestly and lovingly without superiority. Speech unaligned with love happens when you lie to protect your image, judge another to ensure your superiority, create inaccuracies that fit your story, get folks on your side, give unsolicited feedback, or set yourself apart from certain groups of people (including via bigotry) through your language. Also, speaking in Buddhist or psychological terms during painful situations rings of dishonesty when heartfelt communication or a warm hug is called for. Talking (including asking for information) about sensitive issues regarding another person who is not present in the room can divide communities.

Body language, such as rolling the eyes, turning away, glaring, or tapping one's feet while a person is talking, can also be harmful communication. Likewise, when silence takes the place of speaking truth, this is a harmful silence. At the same time, words can separate you from your heart-truth, so it is best not to communicate until you are clear of your emotions. A step toward forgiveness and reconciliation is to inform another person that you lied or you were not

Spirit Friends

able to hold his or her secret. Or you could say that you are still practicing how to express yourself with love.

Wise speech is difficult without a wise heart. We don't know what will surface in life, and we are uncertain what will be communicated in the moment. To ease the difficulty, some rely on communication techniques. Although some techniques of wise speech can work for some situations, such techniques may fail when the circumstances do not fit them or they do not provide a heartfelt response to the situation.

Communication is crucial to sustaining interrelationship between us. Buddha's truth was demonstrated by how he lived his life and emerged in what he *communicated* with others.

Buddhists are practitioners of truth, meaning there is a commitment to the wisdom that arises from our lives. Our truth is not Buddha's truth. Our truth emerges when we awaken to our own life. Truth, along with integrity, emerges from experiencing suffering and discovering the way out of suffering. The truth that emerges in such a way will come through to others in how we move in the world, including how we speak. With this precept, we are called to discover our deepest truths from deep within our bones.

Avoid intoxicants or deliberate loss of awareness; instead, commit to being awake and aware. Buddha was specifically referring to the use of any substances that would alter consciousness and cause confusion. In today's time, these substances could be a myriad of things, from alcoholic beverages to legal and illegal drugs, sex, or even sitting at the computer or TV and being entertained for hours. Even what appears to be good, such as meditation, yoga, or spiritual rituals, can turn into cravings or addictions if it is mistaken for an *external* elixir of comfort or sedation from the chaos of life. Once the habit is developed, the awareness of life is lost, because life is on automatic.

Being an unconscious consumer, buying to eliminate discomfort or to fulfill the missing pleasure of life, is a form of deliberately forsaking awareness that is often seen when there are difficult times. Increasingly extreme situations, such as homelessness, financial decline, or a decline in mental and physical health, can lead to intoxicating actions. When one does not feel welcomed in a society or has lost a sense of belonging, there also can be a need to numb the feelings of the situation. Addictions can emerge when one has to deal with being abused, abandoned, rendered invisible, or shut out of the full benefits of life in the midst of systemic oppression. In many cases, there is an insurmountable need to restore dignity (personally and collectively) and to discover the pain underlying habit and addiction. What are you really craving in life? Most important is to be gentle in the discovery of such pain and not exacerbate the condition of intoxication with impatience.

There are five more grave precepts: (6) avoid discussing the faults of others; (7) avoid praising self while slandering others, (8) avoid being stingy or being possessive, (9) avoid ill will (anger), and (10) avoid being disrespectful of spiritual/religious practices. In each one are treasures. In Buddhism we have three treasures, Buddha, Dharma, and Sangha. We take refuge in the wisdom of the teacher, the teachings, and life in community.

🔀 What do people mean by "taking refuge" in Buddha, Dharma, and Sangha?

Taking refuge means ending suffering by fully devoting your life to liberation, or to the Buddha way, which includes devotion to the three treasures, known as Buddha (the awakened state or the teacher), Dharma (the teachings), and Sangha (the community). When you take refuge, you are establishing trust in the treasures or the gifts of life as they appear in your life. And many of us have received spiritual gifts in the form of teachers, teachings, and a community to support us in walking the path.

Taking refuge does not mean that you run away from the world, hiding in the meditation hall or in your bedroom when times are hard. It doesn't mean staying away from certain kinds of people or places. In the days of Buddha, taking refuge had a more literal meaning, and it still does in some traditions today—for monks and nuns who leave home to live in a monastery, devoting their lives to the path. However, throughout the years, as the practice has taken shape in modern times, there are those of us who do not live in a monastery. In such cases, the action of taking refuge has a broader meaning.

When we, as followers of Buddha, say, "I take refuge in Buddha as the perfect teacher," we are honoring (not worshipping) Buddha as a great teacher. At the same time, we are not taking refuge in Buddha the human being, but rather in devotion to the essence of the being, which is the essence of awakening. You awaken to what in your life is teaching you about life. Buddha clearly saw the nature of things. He did not see with his eyes. He did not use his feet to find the path. He did not formulate an intellectual awareness while probing the mysteries of life. He simply allowed himself to be a vehicle by which unadulterated wisdom poured forth. This was awakening. So when we take refuge in Buddha, we are devoting ourselves to awakening in such a way.

When we say, "I take refuge in Dharma as the perfect teachings," we are taking refuge in what Sensei Dainin Katagiri called good medicine—the teachings. Dharma is the path of life. At the same time, we are taking in *all of life* as teachings, secular and sacred, difficult and easy. Often, we discriminate between what we want to happen in our lives and what we don't. Even though we know better, we expect nothing challenging to happen and literally insist on a problem-free life. I'll never forget how once, when I was complaining about the trouble in my life, a Zen teacher told me that the trouble was also the dharma of my life. Whether they come from precisely Buddha's teachings or life teachings, the lessons can be dull or sharp, and they come and go.

I do experience meeting the Dharma as something that you don't do just once. It occurs as often as one is awakened

25

to the suffering and joy of life. So sometimes I say that I heard the Dharma from my mother first, when, at a time I was disappointed by our church members, she said something like this: "You can't look at other peoples' lives and decide if you are going to pray or not." In other words, if I judge a spiritual or religious practice by its people, I would never practice, because there are no perfect people. It was a lesson I still hold onto today. Human beings are human beings, and *other* people have very little to do with how far I go down a chosen path of awakening.

On the other hand, I might say that Martin Luther King Jr. was a Dharma teacher for me. His message of nonviolence and peace sank deep into my eleven-year-old heart and was especially meaningful at that time, 1963, when four little girls my age had been bombed to death in Alabama because they were black.

Therefore, taking refuge in the Dharma means relating to everything, no matter how tragic, and when we do, everything in life becomes the path by which we discover our true nature. We cannot rely on books and teachers to guide us on every step of the path. Through a direct experience of our own life, not just Buddha's, we come to an awakening steeped in living.

When we say, "I take refuge in Sangha as the perfect life," we are embracing spiritual friendship and the community of those who have devoted themselves to the teachings of Buddha. Buddhists say "perfect life" because to be a part of a community (any community) is to be fully supported on the path of liberation. Community is an expression of our interrelatedness. When the Buddha spoke of Sangha, he was addressing the monks and, later, the nuns. Today, Sangha includes all communities, ordained and nonordained, that practice Buddha's teachings together.

In Sangha, everyone has come together with an expressed willingness to deal with their suffering and its impact on others. There is an expectation that all will be good in the land of meditation. We expect the ground beneath Sangha to be stable and strong when, in truth, we are together in the confusion and challenge of living awake. One day things are one way, and the next a relationship has changed. You feel you've made a mistake, and you begin to blame your discomfort on the forms, the Sangha members, or the teachers. Even though all experiences are valid, they still need investigation. This investigation can be carried out in the midst of the troubled souls, the Sangha, you have chosen to commune with. You could leave and find another community, but what happens for you when the earth begins to shake beneath the new Sangha in the same way as it did underneath the Sangha you left?

Many who take on the practice decide to practice alone. Perhaps their workplace, family, or other communities serve as Sangha. However, the difficulty with such Sangha is that the path of awakening can be unclear, or there may be no conscientious effort on the part of others to walk a path of awakening with you. You may not have the support you need to follow the teachings you have embraced.

In Sangha based on the teachings, you are reminded that you are not alone on the journey. At the same time, I have felt alone in Sangha. I have felt different than the others, and many times this difference stood out in a way that was uncomfortable. Then it was time for me to remember that everyone's path is different. There is no one with exactly the same path as my own. So how do I respond to the uncomfortable situations?

Our Sangha friends are there to assist us by reflecting back to us the ways in which we respond to the events of life. This reflection doesn't mean that these friends are to sit in judgment of our actions or inform us of any wrongdoings. The reflection is silent. It is in the way we see ourselves in each other. When a friend falters or experiences discomfort, we, in turn, are there to witness the faltering and the discomfort, sensing the familiarity of their situation in our own life. When a Sangha member is happy, we see the joy in our own lives.

Many have said to me that they do not need Sangha. My response has been, "Then where will you go when you begin to experience liberation? Who will know the journey you have taken and your vow to be awake?"

☨☨ What is mindfulness?

When your mind is wandering through the past or in the future, you are not engaged in the present. You are not in the place you are sitting or walking in. You are not listening to the person speaking to you. All of your present actions are bound up in the past, or you are planning for the next moment, the next action. Perhaps you are working out in your mind a way to protect yourself from the results of a past experience, or maybe you are thinking up a defense for your actions and your reputation. Or maybe you are worried about what others will say about you, or you're trying to avoid making a mistake in the moment by being one step ahead or worried about lagging far behind. Perhaps you're trying to satisfy a thirst for wealth, love, intimacy, and/or belonging by strategizing about the future. Your emotions may be spinning you into more stories to tell. Your mind is not where you are.

As a result of the suffering we face, everyday mindfulness is difficult. We find ourselves saying, "Hindsight is twenty-twenty," meaning our vision is better now than at the time the harmful actions took place or in the midst of difficult events.

Mindfulness helps us see clearly in the moment of all our actions.

In the mindfulness traditions, such as the Theravada forest tradition and the tradition of Vietnamese Zen teacher Thich Nhat Hanh, there are *gathas* (small verses of prayers) to help us develop mindfulness. Each verse is connected to the simple actions we take daily. Our larger, mindful actions in the world begin in this simple way: when we see, we are seeing; when we walk, we are walking; when we listen, we are listening; when we talk, we are talking—and while we are doing these things, we do nothing else.

Here is a *gatha* for waking up:

Waking up this morning, I smile
24-brand new hours are all for me
I vow to live them mindfully
and look upon all beings with eyes of compassion and love.

For more such gathas see *Present Moment, Wonderful Moment*, by Thich Nhat Hanh.

The following are four gathas from Thich Nhat Hanh's Zen tradition of mindfulness that can be used in our daily life the same way as the gathas mentioned above.

Breathing in, I calm my body.
Breathing out, I smile.
Dwelling in the present moment,
I know this is a wonderful moment.

Breathing in, I am aware of my whole body,
Breathing out, I am aware of my whole body.

Breathing in, I see myself as a flower.
Breathing out, I feel fresh.
Breathing in, I see myself as a mountain.
Breathing out, I feel solid.
Breathing in, I feel myself as still water.
Breathing out, I reflect things as they are.
Breathing in, I see myself as space.
Breathing out, I feel free.
Breathing in, I know that I am breathing in.
Breathing out, I know that I am breathing out.
Breathing in, I know I am breathing in.
Breathing out, I know I am breathing out.

Breathing in, I know I am breathing in.
Breathing out, I know I am breathing out.
As my in-breath grows deep,
My out-breath grows slow.
Breathing in makes me calm.
Breathing out brings me ease.
With the in-breath, I smile,
With the out-breath I release.
Dwelling in the present moment,
I know this is a wonderful moment.

Feelings come and go, like clouds in a windy sky.
Conscious breathing is my anchor.

33 What are compassion, forgiveness, and reconciliation in the context of the Dharma?

To have **compassion** is to care deeply for living beings and to have reverence for all life. Compassion may be accompanied with a strong sense of wanting to do something about the suffering in the world. However, you must have an experience of compassion for yourself before you can be compassionate toward another. Can you accept who you are? Can you accept your actions that may have caused harm to yourself or others?

The most difficult times to be compassionate are when a person does something you find hard to accept or when you love those who are unwilling to return such love. In the face of not receiving love or in the face of rejection, **forgiveness** becomes critical for continuing the path of compassion.

To forgive or not to forgive is a choice of being free or not. Yet forgiveness is not meant to just unburden us of our pain. It is an evolutionary journey into the willingness to forever let go of anger, violence, prejudice, bitterness, and revenge. In the midst of our greatest hurt and pain, to forgive is to see that we all struggle and act out when we are confused or filled with debilitating emotions.

Forgiving is not only an action that takes place *after* the regrettable events. Right in the middle of the events, we can forgive by pausing when we hear the voice in our heads say, "I've been wronged." In the pause, we can see ourselves and/ or the other person struggling with past life experiences in the present moment. Many of us have difficult lives, and it is important to understand how living beings are challenged in the world. With forgiveness, our intention would be to disrupt any further suffering in the moment. To rely on forgiveness as a way out of responsibility is to live an apologetic life. If you frequently say, "I'm sorry," it is time to take a serious look at first forgiving yourself—"I didn't know a better way at the time."

When we can pause and see the root of suffering, we are ready for **reconciliation.** In reconciliation, we reach the place where we are willing to look softly upon another. We are willing to abandon stories, rumors, and gossip. We are willing to sit face-to-face, explore, and work through misunderstanding and discrimination. To enter reconciliation is to say, "I understand," or "I am willing," or "I am willing to not judge." We let go of what we think is real and open to another person's understanding. Once there is reconciliation, we understand that we are one and of each other. The

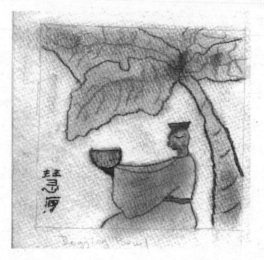

Begging Bowl

Sangha, or community, of those around us can help us by not speaking their opinions of a situation after reconciliation. The situation is laid down as a prayer and left. Compassion, forgiveness, and reconciliation require an intimacy with suffering within your life. In my experience, such intimacy softens the heart and prepares you for heart-work in the world. Once your heart softens, you realize, perhaps, that you were on fire. You realize that you were a human being with the desire to be seen for who you are. Who are you? How does your fire appear? You may discover that the nature of your fire is to:

- Blame others (even though others are involved—interrelated suffering)

- Hold strong opinions about what others should be doing to make things right

- Hold onto anger to justify your mistakes

- Need an apology before you can let go

- Feel the injustices of the culture being repeated and have not found a way to respond that brings well-being to all

- Try to hide a weakness

- Hold folks hostage, unwilling to let others off the hook

- Feel your story is the best reason such and such a thing has happened

- Are unwilling to be the bad guy (when truly there is no bad guy)

- Confuse past wounding experiences with the present situation

- Have difficulty with unpredictable circumstances causing you to move too fast to certainty

- Have expectations of others that they are unaware of

These are only some of the ways we encounter fire with ourselves. If we can understand the nature of these fires or understand fire as nature, we can understand suffering and, therefore, transform it into the water of compassion, forgiveness, and reconciliation. We burn away the walls between us.

What is this burning away and arising from the ashes in Buddhist practice?

In "Fire of Transformation," from spiritual writer, poet, and philosopher Mark Nepo wrote about the nature of fire the way I have experienced it in the context of Buddha's path. He said:

> *Those who know the land say there are good fires that let the soil regenerate. It's a hard lesson but this is true of who we are. And I confess, who I am has burned to the ground more than once. Though it's still too early to tell if these were good fires or not. What keeps us going, thank God, is how we hold each other long enough to burn off what is unnecessary and how we save each other when the fire starts to take too much. You could say this is where the fire of God meets the fire of Love. When we hold each other to the heat till the illusions we reach for, burn. When we soothe each other as the heart is freed of what*

35

*it dreams of, long enough to discover the raw beauty of what
has always been there. When we set aflame the many selves we
try on along the way, we trip back into the naked self we first
arrived with. All this I saw when burning up, the instant you
pulled me from the fire of my own making.*

In the Nichiren Buddhist tradition, I was taught that to
practice with the vows of a bodhisattva, a spiritual warrior,
is to practice as if your head were on fire. I feel that being
a follower of Buddha is like entering one fire after another
because we have committed ourselves to being awake.

So what does this mean, this being on fire, this burning?
Nepo says that there are good fires that let the soil regener-
ate. I feel he is speaking of those experiences in life that are
difficult, yet that transform us, creating new land, regener-
ated territory in which we continue to live our lives. He is
saying we have places in our lives that get sparked, then a
fire begins and we burn until there is nothing left but the
ashes, another form of the fire. In this transformation, there
is regeneration. The ash is soft ground for compassion, reconciliation, and forgiveness.

In the indigenous African cosmology, fire is the element
of origin, the element that was present at the beginning;
it is the state to which everything eventually returns, the
state the ancestors are in. To the West African Dagara tribe,
according to Malidoma Somé, a Dagara spiritual teacher,
fire opens the door to our awareness. We find the element of
fire mentioned in many spiritual teachings. Buddha himself
delivered what was called the Fire Sermon *(Adittapariyaya
Sutra)*. In that teaching, he talked about fire as suffering.

36

He said all of life is burning. Therefore, being on fire, this burning, appears to be the nature of living, a part of how we experience life. The burning can be destructive or transformative. I had an experience of such burning away, and up from the ashes flew butterflies.

When I attended my first three-week meditation intensive, there was sitting and walking meditation for six hours a day for three weeks. Layers of my life melted away each week. In the burning, there was fear, anger, restlessness, and disconnection from others. I began to wrestle with my mother in my mind. I was a child receiving her rage through the lashings of her belt. Each day of the sesshin, the same movie with my mother and me went through my mind. I could not understand how she could both love and hurt me. After two weeks of sitting meditation, this burning continued to leave me nauseated and dizzy. Finally, toward the end of the intensive, as I was sitting near a window, I began to see that little girl, little Earthlyn. I saw her unfold as a butterfly, soft, floating, beautiful. I cried, realizing that I had been working hard at not being that butterfly, so vulnerable, so soft, afraid of being smashed.

In seeing the butterfly, I knew that I could not care deeply for anyone until I could feel that softness. In the silence, I understood the anger of my mother as her fear. I could see how her living in difficult times in Louisiana in the early 1900s had created a hard shell around her loving heart. I could see that she was a human being, with all the suffering of any other person. After having these realizations, I could smile with her and talk about the ways in which she affected how I walked the earth. As my own rage and softness merged together, I could see that I was certainly my mother's daughter.

I walked slowly to my room in the Zen center and wrote a poem titled "See the Butterfly," which expressed an innate compassion and forgiveness for, and reconciliation with, my mother and those who I felt hurt me in my lifetime. What I felt my mother didn't see was what I knew myself to be when the fire within was burned away into ashes. "See the Butterfly" is not a poem demanding visibility or one of complaining of what folks don't see in me, but one in which my inner spirit affirms the seeing that one cannot do with the eyes. The poem ends with a reminder that the breeze touches each of us as we touch each other.

No one has ever told me that I remind them of a butterfly,
bearing up in the wild winds,
migrating through thick tight seasons,
arriving, still, light enough to rest on the underside of
a leaf.

And that soft sand hill crane,
that spreads its wings in order to land safely, is no different than me;
but I am hardly ever seen that way.

I feel like a water lily, resting face up in the middle of a
sunny day,
stretching gloriously out from the center to the edge of
the world, eventually, leaving fossils of myself against
the muddied earth;
wondering have I been seen?

That mourning dove,
flying above contradictions,
arising from its wounds,
echoes the songs hidden in the caves of my heart.

And when there are orchids, I see myself,
facing up, darkness filled with light,
choosing to be fuchsia, lavender and yellow,
coming up from the middle of the earth where ancestors have come before me;
hoping that someone sees my beauty.

And no, no one has said to me that I remind them of a rose,
a red maple leaf,
a hummingbird,
or a simple blade of grass standing in precious soil, rich
and well.
Oh, how I wish, that when you feel a breeze move quietly across your face, that it would remind you of us.

⛩ What is wisdom?

Compassion and wisdom are talked about as two wings
of a bird. Through compassion, wisdom emerges, and the
spirit takes flight. Wisdom is understanding the interrelationship between all things—understanding that, in fact,
Zenju Earthlyn, butterflies, sandhill cranes, maple leaves,
and blades of grass are integrated within a life-affirming
web of nature.

Wisdom is knowing by heart that the weave of nature includes everyone and everything. Wisdom comes up through our awareness of life. Wisdom cannot be taught or gained from reading books—not even this book. But there are created situations in which wisdom about our lives can emerge, such as meditation retreats or rituals such as vision quests in the wilderness. However, in order to gain wisdom through these means, we would have to spend a great part of our lives dedicated to such spiritual work.

In essence, a river of wisdom takes *devotion* to clear seeing and witnessing life. When you surrender after great perseverance, and you are so tired from such hard work, then you might begin to transmit light into the world.

What about the teaching that all things are impermanent?

The reason one cannot hold onto things, relationships, and stories, as they exist in the moment, is that there is impermanence *(anicca)* in all phenomena. Everything changes from moment to moment, even if we can't see the change happening.

There have been a few times in my life when I could not feed or house myself without help from friends and family. During one of these times, I took a walk around the neighborhood. I paused at a garden of roses that I had passed many times without stopping. Although there were many lovely roses, I chose one of them to smell and study.

I observed each fold. Though the rose was changing right before my eyes, I could not see the change with my eyes. There were no outside signs of its imminent death. I knew then that the difficult time I was having was also changing and that it would eventually come to an end in a way that I could not see in the moment.

Good times are subject to impermanence as well. Joy arises and ceases in many cycles, and yet we expect every moment of our lives to be joyous. Many of us strategize making "good" causes in our lives so that we receive "good" effects. We give generously hoping to receive the same in return. We help out those in need hoping to be seen as a "good" person. In essence, we are basing our giving and receiving on conditions that would personally benefit our own lives. However, the universal law of cause and effect cannot be manipulated in such a way. Underlying all of life is impermanence. We don't know what is ahead, so it is not so easy to control our lives with what we give or how much of ourselves we give. We can only be guided by our inner wisdom. All conditions for giving love or being compassionate are to be abandoned because conditions change moment to moment. On the path, we learn to live with uncertainty.

Some of us become aloof and say, "Why bother to do anything if we have so little control?" We must still take action in our lives, but with room for a result that might be different than what we expect. I didn't expect to encounter Buddha's teachings in my life, but I did.

What do Buddhists believe?

Buddha taught to avoid becoming attached to beliefs, to not grasp onto what we think, because what we think can cause great illusions and unbearable isolation. Instead of believing, what I practice is seeing—but not with my eyes. When I see with my heart that which is around me, wisdom and awareness surface, rather than a fixation with what my *mind* believes in regard to what I see.

For example, if I see an apple pie on the table, my belief could be that food comes from a store. But when I see with my heart, I see the apple. I see the stem from the apple hung from the apple tree. I see the seed in the apple. Around the core of the apple, I may see the earth from which the tree emerged. In this seeing, I can touch the apple tree and the sun in my heart.

Therefore, teachings in Buddhism are not beliefs as much as they are principles or universal laws based on the nature of things and not what we perceive.

What are Zen and zazen?

While Zen has its origins in Taoism and Chinese Ch'an, there are many kinds of Zen traditions, including Soto, Rinzai, Sanbo Kyodan, Obaku, Shaolin Kungfu, and Vietnamese and Korean Zen. Within each tradition there are various Zen rituals, forms, and chants based on the many lineages within each tradition. As a result, there is no one kind of Zen, which gives rise to many meanings of Zen and interpretations of the practice.

The word *Zen* has fallen into the North American vocabulary as an adjective for anything in which breathing is referred to, anything resembling something from the Eastern continents, or a word synonymous with tranquility. I have heard "That's very Zen" as a comment on minimalism in speech, calm behavior, home décor, or food. I have no particular concern for such uses and actually enjoy it when the word is used at all. However, there is a more accurate context of Zen of which I am sure most folks have some clue.

Zen is the Japanese reference to what the Chinese call Ch'an Buddhism. Ch'an is Chinese for the Sanskirt word

Buddha to Buddha

∂hyāna which refers to meditative absorption in which dualities such as I/you, dark/light, true/false are eliminated. Historically Zen as a religion can be traced back to Bodhidharma's transmission of Ch'an in China during the 6th and 7th century. And yet, Zen is not a religion in the sense that each individual has his or her own experience of the practice.

Zen teaches the practice of *zazen*. Zazen is the Japanese word used for silent sitting meditation. Zazen is an effort to practice wakeful attention without directing or clinging to one's thoughts. Zazen is just sitting or shikantaza as we call it in Zen practice.

Zazen is the Japanese word used for meditation in the tradition of Soto Zen. Za means to sit down and Zen refers to silent meditation. *Zazen* is sitting meditation.

The meaning of *Zen*, by its very essence, require a relationship to life experience. Therefore, the meaning of *Zen* is more accurate when applied to the lives we live. When you ask, "What is Zen?" you are asking, "What are you?" or "Who are you?"

Zen is to study the self. Eihei Dogen, founder of the Soto school of Zen in thirteenth-century Japan, wrote, "To study the Buddha Way is to study the self, to study the self is to forget the self, to forget the self is to be enlightened by the ten thousand things . . ." When he said "forget the self," he didn't mean to enter a self-imposed amnesia or to be unconscious of being human, but rather to untangle ourselves from what we believe is "real" about each other and the world around us.

The late Shunryu Suzuki Roshi, founder of the San Francisco Zen Center, said, "Zen is Zen when you are Zen." He means that Zen is the complete path of awakening within your life. Zen is a lived experience.

33 What is happening during meditation?

The simple answer is breathing. To breathe is to live. The majority of practitioners of Buddha's teachings chant, though very few traditions have meditation at the center of their practice.

Many people see Buddhism as a meditation practice for those seeking tranquility and a calm mind. When I meditate, life slows down, and what I experience in meditation is not always calm. There can be much distress. I breathe, in and out, becoming aware of what, in my mind and body, hinders compassion, love, and wisdom. With that awareness, I can breathe again, in and out, through the hindrances of fear and desire, signaling the mind and body to let go of whatever story fuels the fear and desire.

In the past, I lived much of my life following the voices of other people without listening to my own heart, and also grasping for things outside of myself. In living in such a way, I lost track of the true nature of life. This loss resulted in mental, physical, financial, emotional, and spiritual despair. An unawakened heart-mind tends to perpetuate itself. Meditation helps to illuminate such embedded consciousness. In the silence, something of myself is stripped away, and I am left standing with a new emptiness. Juan Ramón Jiménez's poem "Seas" says it best:

> I feel my boat
> has struck something large
> there, in the depths of the sea!
>
> And then nothing
> happens! Nothing . . . Silence . . . Waves . . .
>
> Nothing happens? Or has everything happened
> And are we now, calm, in someplace new?

In general, when you meditate, the mind flows in a stream of thoughts in one direction toward the breath—not thinking or pondering anything. As the wave of thoughts goes by, you eventually lose your identification with happiness or misery. In that loss, there is purification and an experience of Buddha nature, and there is a newness to the moment and to life. Jesus Christ said, "Blessed are the pure in heart, for they shall see God." Experiencing purification or Buddha nature is similar to becoming "pure in heart."

As many traditions as there are in Buddhism, there are as many ways to meditate, to reach the silence or the tranquility where nothing and everything happens.

Meditation is source of creative engagement, which means meditation is a total experience of life with each breath, each moment. Meditation is also an experience of awakening. To awaken our relationships with each living being is an act of love for oneself and for others. When we sit in meditation we turn the light inward with our breath. The light enables us to see how we engage with others, with life. In meditation practice we breathe in and breathe out, we allow the thoughts to pass through our minds, one after the other. To stop and dwell on any thought is to give it fuel and interrupt the flow of breath in and out. Caution: the brain is built to think, so you cannot stop the thinking. Instead, you recognize the scurrying of thoughts and use the breath to slow down their race through the many shadowy places within our minds.

Some sit upright in chairs, and others sit on meditation cushions. In zazen, our eyes are slightly open, and we gaze downward while facing a blank wall. We lay the left hand inside of the right hand, and our thumb tips touch as if we

were holding an egg. But it is a raw egg, so we have to find a balance of holding it not too tightly and not too loosely. When our thumbs collapse or fall away from each other, we have entered a dream state or have fallen asleep. Our thumbs remind us to breathe gently, but stay awake, creating an alert relaxation. Our shoulders are down, and the tongue is touching the roof of the mouth. Our chins are tucked in, and the top of the head is up, as if a string were pulling us up from the top of our head. In this posture of concentration, we are learning to breathe in the midst of life's distractions. Someone may cough, walk by, snore, cry. Whatever happens in the zendo (or meditation hall), we breathe in and breathe out.

Sometimes there is a quiet calm; other times the unbearable surfaces, and you can become confused with the things of the world. Meditation cannot address all of our emotional issues; therefore, I recommend seeking other healing paths available to you. At the same time, I found it helpful to have a teacher or senior practitioner who knows the teachings to help with what surfaces in meditation or point out what is obstructing the view of freedom. Therefore, whenever possible, attend sitting retreats for support. Connect with other folks who practice the teachings of Buddha.

With Tibetan Buddhist meditation, you may be guided by visualizations. In some practices, you are given objects to concentrate on, such as a scroll with a mantra or a bell to remind you to be mindful. In Soto Zen, we face the wall in silence, without anyone guiding us in visualizations. What arises will arise and cease. We are not just being quiet or still. In facing the wall, we develop our ability to concentrate with the breath while staying awake to the life that is passing by. We are allowing wisdom to come forth and becoming aware of what needs to be healed in us.

There is a saying in the Zen world: "Zazen (sitting meditation) is good for nothing." I didn't understand that saying because I wanted something back for meditating hour after hour. I wanted to instantly eliminate *all* of my suffering. Then one day, after sitting for an hour, I grew tired working hard at pushing the suffering away. As a matter of fact, I suffered more by trying to work with the suffering in such a way. Finally, after my exhaustion from working so hard, there was nothing but sitting. I had to sit and trust that all would be revealed without any strategy. In that case, zazen was good for such nothingness. In other words, there are many meditation techniques, but these techniques alone will not serve as the infinite mirror you will need to see your true nature.

⊠⊠ What is true nature?

When we perceive things as separate or fragmented, we are not seeing the true nature of things. When we perceive at all, using our intellectual mind to know something or someone, we are not seeing the true nature of all things. True nature is beyond perception, conceptualization, or any human conditioning that has been shaped since our birth. As a result of true nature's primordial sense, it is hard to grasp or explain. You cannot know true nature without being awakened to all that surrounds you. In many instances, true nature is talked about as Buddha nature (*Buddha-dhātu*, or *Bussho* in Zen).

True nature is not to be mistaken for being real versus being phony or unreal. The teaching is addressing how things come into being and live from moment to moment. There is a continuum and interrelationship of living beings, which includes the sun, moon, stars, trees, all that supports the constant coming and going of things and life. Our true nature is that we are nobody, going nowhere (the classic title of Ayya Khema's book). We can say we are such and such, but who are we? We can say we are from a particular country, but the country cannot be our true nature. We are like fire that comes into being. We take shape as the earth has done. We dissolve. And we do this together moment after moment. This is the true nature of our lives.

Does meditation take away emotions such as anger, jealousy, or sadness?

Disturbances, harmful situations, and challenging people can all be assistants in deepening the walk of life. Many expect all Buddhists to be nice or something along those lines. Some enter Buddhist centers hoping to become as nice as they think all Buddhists are. They may think, "If only I could get rid of my rage, life would be good, and everyone would love me because I am so nice."

Of course, this thought is as ungrounded as it sounds. We enter Buddha's path as human beings, and we walk on it as human beings. We are guaranteed to feel, fully, all of the emotions of a human being. What the path assists us in doing is *seeing the root of the emotion* in the midst of its occurrence, so that the response is not more pain and suffering. We learn to question, "What is going on here?"

During one of my stays in a monastery, I experienced great pain when fellow practitioners could not accept my invisible physical disability as the reason I could not kneel to serve the meals or stand in the kitchen for very long. The frustration others received and the isolation I felt as results of my physical challenges fueled my sense of rejection and not belonging. I would sit in the zendo (meditation hall) and receive spontaneous visions of myself in a bright yellow robe amidst the black robes of Soto Zen that we were required to wear.

After weeks of sensing the angst from others and holding a desire for the agitated few to change their focus, I began to suffer. During the *oryoki* meals (a ceremonial way of eating in the zendo), I could hardly swallow my food because of the need to burst into tears. Soon, the wailing inside me broke down to small weepings every time we had a forty-minute sitting session.

Finally, I requested guidance from the lead teacher. I explained to him what was happening. He listened without ever taking his eyes off of me. After I was done speaking, he said, "All emotions are from the past." I blinked once, then twice. How could that be? I thought to myself. He asked me to return to the zendo and to let those feeling come forward until I could see with my heart what was going on with me and not the others.

I returned and continued to weep in my seat until one day during lunch, I could not take another bite. I put down my utensils and allowed the tears to gush forward. While they were coming, a vision of myself emerged in one of my dresses I wore at the age of eight. It was plaid with puffed sleeves, starched stiff, the way my mother ironed our dresses. I had white anklet socks and black patent leather, buckled shoes. My hair was pressed straight and pulled tight in two ponytails, one on each side of my head, with bangs that rolled under. Suddenly, in the zendo, I was the little Earthlyn who had been forced to attend a predominantly white Jewish elementary school in Los Angeles in the early 1960s. I was there, right at the desk of my elementary school instead of in my seat in the zendo. I felt the old anger of being called names, being pushed, being different. I felt the jealousy I had for my best friend, Roslyn, who belonged at the school because she was Jewish. I felt all the emotions possible while sitting in meditation.

Although the incidents that occurred at the monastery were new events of my life, the emotions were clearly from events long gone. I understood those events of the past to be what shaped the suffering for me in the zendo. I allowed the tears to continue for days. For three months, we sat anywhere from five to six hours a day, every day. I had plenty of time to look into the infinite mirror of zazen and see the life renamed Zenju.

Once the emotions rode themselves out, I was able to deal with the situation at hand. I could address the present-day problem in the zendo without getting back at the boy at my elementary school who stole my berets, or the boy who spit in my face in junior high school. I was more effective in practicing complete and loving speech at the Zen Center—not because I had any technique for wise speech, but because I had completely surrendered to my heart.

The pain of the present-day events at the monastery did not go away because healing is a work in progress. I continued such healing, weeping day by day. If I had turned my attention away from the purification occurring within and turned toward those who were focusing on me, I would have missed a powerful chance for transforming suffering in my life. I did not become a stoic practitioner so that I would be seen as a powerful mountain sitting atop my meditation cushion. I was a tearful Zen student who saw clearly that my journey on the path required feeling and seeing every step of the way, without the stories. We are to be full human beings on the path of Buddha, with all of the emotions of a human being. We cannot fully practice such a call for liberation without our lives being fully exposed. There is no hiding.

33 Are all actions in Buddhism about the self? What about the effects of others on our lives?

I have heard many folks say, "That's not about me. It's your stuff." And when I began my practice in the Nichiren tradition, that's what the teachers *appeared* to be telling me.

I went to a teacher to complain about a roommate. The first thing she said was, "Why are you so arrogant?" I started to explain to her again that this roommate was the problem, not me. She laughed and repeated her comment, adding, "You think you're better and that you're right." I looked around the room as if someone were playing a joke on me. I thought to explain it for the third time, but instead I sat quietly, upset that she didn't just agree with me.

I was eventually excused and directed to chant until the mirror of my life was illuminated. Therefore, I chanted the Lotus Sutra (the practice in Nichiren Buddhism) for hours, hoping to get this roommate to behave. Instead of ways to control the roommate, what came forward was a reflection of myself. I began to list in my head the things I didn't like about this roommate. The first thing on the list was that she was arrogant in the same way that the teacher had said I was. I kept chanting, and then before I could get through thirty minutes of chanting, there was a laundry list of what I didn't like about this roommate. As I began to write them down so I wouldn't forget, *I realized the behaviors listed were the very things I secretly did not like about myself.* The reflection finally had revealed my roommate's face to be my own.

This mirroring did not mean that the roommate was no longer a problem for me. But what the practice showed me was that everything in my life and in the world is a mirror reflection of our inner lives. It revealed that while other's lives impact our own, the responses to such effects still lie within our own life.

We can only study our own life in the infinite mirror that we polish with our spiritual work. We can only look deeply from where we stand on the path. We cannot find Buddha's path with his feet and eyes. We surely cannot find it within another person's body.

You have only this life. Therefore, Buddha's teachings address the life you are living, the precious gift you received long ago.

33 What about chanting?

Chanting is as ancient as the Aka and Baka people (known as Pygmies) in the fading rainforest of the Congo. Their chants are as old as 8,000 to 10,000 years. Likewise, in every tradition of Buddhism, there are chants as old as

3,000 years. Chanting is *active* meditation. Chanting is the vibrational aspect of the Dharma, where harmony and well-being are articulated by sounds. The chants have specific purposes, such as to arouse compassion, to honor someone who has died, or to uplift. It is not necessary to know the meaning of the words beforehand; we just need to be willing to sink into the rhythm as a unifying force within. Soto Zen chants include a chant of the lineage of ancestors from Buddha to the present, meal chants, well-being chants, chants for repentance of ancient karma, chants for death, and more.

When I first started to chant in the Nichiren tradition, my throat and neck were so tight that my ears hurt as I chanted. The pain made it clear to me that chanting acted as a fine indicator of tension or relaxation, or whether I was breathing or not. Eventually, as I learned to relax my body, my chest opened as the sounds moved from the pit of my stomach (the *hara*) out into the sacred hall. I could breathe.

I felt the chants grace my thick lips and felt that my southern Louisiana ancestors knew that all was well with their African daughter chanting in Pali, Sanskit, ancient Chinese, and Japanese. It was all very natural to me. As I chanted, chills went through my body in the same way they did when I sang the hymns in the Church of Christ. There was an immediate recognition of rhythm moving away the things weighing down my heart. My mind and body were in one present moment with the breath. Chanting opened my heart.

When I'm chanting the rhythm of dharma and emotional paralyzing thoughts interrupt the chant, I start speaking the words stuck in my brain. I lose my place in the chant. The chant stops, and then I have to begin again. Then, at times, I can feel the emotional fullness of the chants opening my heart. For these reasons, the state of mind is more important than the sound of your voice while chanting. It is the one heart-mind of the chanters that creates a soothing experience for someone listening to any kind of chanting.

Chanting in rhythm with others, each of us offering our rhythmic contribution, is an act of interdependence. When a neighbor stops to take a breath, someone else picks up the phrase until it is his or her turn to inhale or exhale. When we all surrender to the sound of chanting, when there is no I that is chanting, a beautiful thing can happen between us. At the point of surrender, there is no judgment and no thinking, because the whole experience has moved beyond thought. In essence, chanting can be an authentic expression of being fully present.

Likewise, when I am drumming with my African drums, if my mind is not on just drumming, I miss out on the experience of the pure, liberating action of drumming. When I breathe deep into the rhythm, listening, having nothing to do with the voice or the expression of the drum in the moment, experiencing no ego, I feel as though I am conveying my innermost being—a soul that loves to speak, laugh, and weep. So the emotion is there, but in a divine expression rather than a paralyzing experience of fear, anger, and confusion.

❧❧ Do some people have good karma and some people have bad karma?

Karma means intentional action, past and present. Buddha was specifically concerned with actions of the body, mind, and speech. The result of your intentional actions is *vipaka*. What we call bad and good karma includes both—karma, the action, and vipaka, the result of the action. Most times we do not remember our actions (karma), but we often suffer the result (vipaka) of our actions. So when we feel righteous and say to someone, "It's your karma," it is more accurate to say, "It's your karma *and* vipaka."

The fact that actions can have good and bad results does not mean there are good and bad people.

To change your karma or actions you take in life, you would have to transform your motivations or intentions. What motivates you to say a particular thing to someone? What made you get up and leave the room? What motivated you to express your thoughts at a particular time and place? These questions help us to witness our actions so that we can transform our suffering.

There are many books that can help you understand karma. I suggest *The Path with Heart* by Jack Kornfield.

❧❧ What about God?

I know God to be love. And I know there is love and faith at the root of Buddha's teachings. Specifically, in many Buddhist traditions, there are deities, but in modern Nichiren and Soto Zen, there is no one personified god to whom we give over our burdens of life. In Buddhist tradition, there is no one god that liberates us from suffering.

External objects such as statues of Buddha, scrolls, Tibetan flags, or Tibetan *thankas* (Buddhist paintings used for meditation) are meant to bring out what is inside of you. We do not worship these objects. There is no reliance on anything external for intervention. Likewise, teachers are not to be worshipped or do not act as conduits to God, but are spiritual assistants to guide us on the path. There is no worship of ancestors or deities, as the essence the entities represent is within our very bones. So when we chant the names of Buddha's ancestors, we are calling their awakening forth from within.

Buddha's teachings—from India to Thailand, from China to Japan, from Korea to Vietnam, and beyond—have taken on the shape of the people, the times, and the places they have reached, as has every other spiritual practice or religious philosophy. In contemporary times, the teachings are taking shape in South America, Africa, and the United States. Yet in this reshaping of an ancient path, most of Buddha's practitioners still do not rely on a personified god. Instead, when life gets rough *and* when it's not so rough, we take refuge in Buddha, Dharma, and Sangha.

Because I was raised in a Christian church populated by black people, God was prominent most of my spiritual life. My parents relied heavily on God. When the enslaved Africans in the United States understood God as a creator of all living beings and on the side of those who experience insurmountable suffering, the enslaved Africans embraced Christ's teachings. To them, Christ was a liberator, and God was just. This notion of God and justice together made black people's Christianity a socially conscious religion, as well as a transformative and liberating one, despite the fact that Christianity was mostly forced upon the slave. In essence, black people's Christianity included personal soul revival/healing and collective freedom.

Would a practice steeped in Buddhism do the same? Better yet, is a Buddhist practice meant to do the same? What about God? There were no simple answers to these questions, but they were important questions in my exploration of Buddha's path. When asked by a teacher what my temple would look like, I replied, "Lots of children, grandparents, food, drumming, flowers, chanting, and plenty of time for silence." The teacher said, "That's just how they do it in Thailand." I smiled, feeling affirmed in my notion of bringing to the practice some cultural aspects of my life that were similar to my Christian upbringing.

❁ Why do we experience so much dissatisfaction as human beings?

We usually see and perceive of each other and the things of the world by appearance. As a consequence, our attention is on the appearance of things and how we appear to others. With an attention to appearance, we all have attachments, repulsion, and cravings for this and that. The cravings come from clinging to what Buddha named the five *skandhas*, or aggregates, that make up a human being. The five skandhas are:

The material body *(rupa)* — "where I am." Ask, "Is this body who I am?"

Feelings *(vedana)* — "how I am." Ask, "Is my heart open despite what I feel?"

Perceptions *(sanna)* — "what I perceive myself to be." Ask, "Am I sure of what I am perceiving?"

Mental formations *(sankhara)* — "why I am acting this way." Ask, "What distortions are blocking my heart?"

Consciousness *(viññana)* — "whereby my experience I am." Ask, "Am I being guided by the wisdom that has emerged in my life or by emotion?"

When clinging to these five aspects, we suffer from dissatisfaction. Our hearts are closed or opened depending on our nature to cling to one thing or another. We are focused on a view of ourselves that is unaligned with Buddha's teachings of interrelationship.

In essence, in suffering we are maintaining the illusion "I am," rather than affirming "We are." Sri Rama Krishna said, "The wave is of the ocean, not the ocean itself." The wave has no independent existence. When we think of ourselves as independent and cling to who we think we are, dissatisfaction arises.

⧓ How can we transform dissatisfaction?

We can develop open-heartedness. We can begin by asking questions about our grasping onto what we believe. Ask, "Is there a way I can let go of, even if for a moment, my own beliefs? Where did such beliefs come from? Past experiences? What if I am not the "I" that I think I am?" Taking time to make such inquiries about your life is a significant step toward ease and contentment.

The next step one can take in dealing with dissatisfaction is to consider the web of life we all share. Consider what has been given and received by your connection to other living beings, including those beings that have sustained your life. Granted, we give and receive things that do not feel good, so at those times we may retreat to our seemingly solitary place in the world. We may even say, "I knew that friendship or relationship wasn't going to work." And yet, even those harsh things in life further indicate that the "I" you cling to is being further shaped by disconnection or continued connection with others.

The third step you might try in beginning a journey to transform dissatisfaction is to intentionally take time to view life without an old story, to walk without thoughts of how you look, to listen without interpretation, to taste something as if for the first time, or to smell and not name what you are smelling. Move through the world without thoughts of liking or disliking this and that.

In following these steps, you are letting go of your automatic way of thinking and behaving. You are leaving room for bending rigidity and melting the hard places within.

In this way, we face *sunyata* (meaning "emptiness" in Pali), the teaching that we have no individual nature, no existence without others, no existence without a cause or condition to what we experience in life. In essence, there is no self-being in and of itself. Within a state of seeing our connectedness, we open our hearts.

In many Buddhist practices we have what is called the Heart Sutra to help cultivate such openness. It is teaching given by Avalokiteshvara Bodhisattva, Buddha of Compassion (who took the shape of the feminine Kuan Yin in China), to the monk Shariputra.

The first time I chanted the Heart Sutra, my heart opened, and I didn't understand the reason. The *kokyo*, one who leads the chants, sounds out the title first, "Heart of Great Perfect Wisdom Sutra" (an English translation of *Maka Hannyu Haramitta Shin Gyo*), and then the body of practitioners begin to chant in unison. The words lifted and moved me somewhere between heaven and earth. We chanted:

Avalokiteshvara Bodhisattva when deeply practicing prajna paramita, clearly saw that all five aggregates are empty and thus relieved all suffering. Shariputra, form does not differ from emptiness, emptiness does not differ from form. Form itself is emptiness, emptiness itself form. Sensations, perceptions, formations, and consciousness are also like this. Shariputra, all dharmas are marked by emptiness; they neither arise nor cease, are neither defiled nor pure, neither increase nor decrease. Therefore, given emptiness, there is no form, no sensation, no perception, no formation, no consciousness; no eyes, no ears, no nose, no tongue, no body, no mind, no sight, no sound, no smell, no taste, no touch, no object of mind, no realm of sight . . . no realm of mind consciousness. There is neither ignorance nor extinction of ignorance . . . neither old age and death, nor extinction of old age and death; no suffering, no cause, no cessation, no path, no knowledge and no attainment. With nothing to attain, a bodhisattva relies on prajna paramita, and thus the mind is without hindrance. Without hindrance, there is no fear. Far beyond all inverted views, one realizes nirvana. All buddhas of past, present, and future rely on prajna paramita and thereby attain unsurpassed, complete, perfect enlightenment. Therefore, know the prajna paramita as the great miraculous mantra, the great bright mantra, the supreme mantra, the incomparable mantra, which removes all suffering and is true, not false. Therefore we proclaim the prajna paramita mantra, the mantra that says: "Gate Gate Paragate Parasamgate Bodhi Svaha."

(Text taken from the chant book at the San Francisco Zen Center.)

I felt the freedom of those words, but didn't understand them. I read the chant repeatedly as if foraging through it for food. Immediately, I wanted to know the meaning of the teaching, the reason for my resonance. After the service, I asked for a copy of the chant. The head of practice, the *tanto*, only smiled at me, as if to say that I could not possess those words. Later, the practice guidance told me to be patient, witness the sensations, and to simply be with not understanding.

It wasn't until later that year, during a Zen training, that I fully understood the Heart Sutra in relationship to the internal emotional pain and suffering I experienced from being born in a dark-skinned body, a second-generation descendant of enslaved Africans in North America. Those teachings on the five skandhas challenged my very existence, who and what I thought myself to be, as well as how I perceived the world. I was asked to consider body and mind in light of what is seen, heard, sensed, and thought of. We were asked to view, with compassion, our clinging and grasping to our perceived humanness as hindrances to our innate wisdom as living beings.

Mother + Child 2

We were encouraged not to take an intellectual or academic journey into this core teaching about the heart, but rather a journey of heart, in which we would seriously examine how we suffer when we grip onto what we think we see, smell, taste, touch, and hear.

At the end of hours of sitting with the journey offered during the training, I felt that the "no" part in the chant was about compassion and not about a vacant emptiness. The "no" meant make no distinction between living beings in regard to who is best and who isn't, what is and what isn't. Without such distinction, compassion can be aroused.

Even though we may never be completely free of our conditioning as human beings, we can be awake to how it impacts our lives together. While being awake seems to be a small effort, it is immense, difficult, and necessary for ending suffering. Because we live by the efforts of all other beings, we must deeply observe all life.

What about women and Buddhism?

From ancient times, there exist seventy-three poems called *Therigatha*. These poems were about women elders or wise women of early Buddhism. Mahapajapati Gotami, the aunt who raised Buddha, was the founder of the first order of Buddhist nuns, which comprised displaced wives, widows, prostitutes, dancers, and musicians. Mahapajapati had to petition many years, walk many miles until her feet bled, protest profusely, shave her head, and put on a saffron robe before her nephew, Buddha, realized that women were worthy of ordination. Shakyamuni Buddha was influenced by cultural beliefs about women during his time. To this day, there is a tension among monks, nuns, priests, women, and men in Buddhist traditions—a tension that is being addressed in many forums and books.

Modern-day Buddhist women, ordained or not, from all continents, have continued in the path of Mahapajapati, persisting on the path of enlightenment for everyone. The women throughout Buddhist history have been liberating presences that have influenced the development of the teachings, rituals, and ceremonies associated with awakening in the way it was taught aeons ago.

Further explorations by women following the path of Buddha will reveal new ways that all beings can coexist. Commentaries on our experience as women are needed so that new teachings are revealed in relationship to the noble truths. As Buddhist women, we are responsible for healing the pain women have suffered since the time of Mahapajapati. What will that healing be, and when will it take place?

For more on the topic of women and Buddhism, I suggest reading *The First Buddhist Women* by Susan Murcott, *Meeting Faith: The Forest Journals of a Black Buddhist Nun* by Faith Adielé, *Dreaming Me: Black, Baptist, and Buddhist—One Woman's Spiritual Journey* by Jan Willis, *Zen Women: Beyond Tea Ladies, Iron Maidens, and Macho Masters* by Grace Schireson and Miriam Levering, *Women of the Way: Discovering 2,500 Years of Buddhist Wisdom* by Sallie Teasdale, and *Buddhism After Patriarchy: A Feminist History, Analysis and Reconstruction of Buddhism* by Rita Gross. *Sky Train: Tibetan Women On the Edge of History* by Canyon Sam.

⚅ How does entering the Buddha way affect our understanding of race, gender, or sexual orientation as the form of our lives?

What is this form, this body, this earth element that would live and then dissolve into the earth? What is this body that, upon death, it doesn't matter whether this body is dark or not?

I imagine that upon death, the emptiness of my body, of this form, will be most obvious. The form has been named, defined, and identified with; yet without another to call the name, speak its story, identify it, there is no form. And yet many of us suffer for the ways in which we are embodied, especially those who are different than the predominant culture in terms of race, gender, sexual orientation, or physical ability.

Buddha taught that the body, when clung to, is dukkha and ultimately dissatisfying. So how does one open to the body itself, when clinging to it is dukkha?

When Buddha taught about the truth of suffering, he described clinging to the body as clinging to that which is perceived as solid and solidified. He went on to name thirty-two body parts and said that if we say these parts belong to us, we have attached and are clinging to the body.

Skin is one of those parts named. And I am thinking about black skin. If I say I belong to black people, therein is the potential for suffering, in the form of the chance of not belonging. When I say I'm black, there again is the potential for suffering, should someone say I'm not acting black or being black. The reason for the potential suffering is that blackness is a perception that is prone to distortion. This is not to say that I do not experience myself as black or African American. But *attaching* and *clinging* to blackness leaves no room for transformation within the context of blackness and no room for new kinds of kinships that might take shape over time. Being black can be empowering, *and* it can perpetuate the self and the limitations that often come with being black. However, at the same time, studying the limitations and boundaries of being black can bring about a quest for a big mind, openness of heart, *and* love.

While grasping at blackness, I am still able to explore how to honor my heritage without causing suffering. I asked myself, how can I experience everyday life in a dark body as a place of liberation?

With this inquiry, (prior to entering Zen practice) I took a week out of my life to visit the Spirit Rock Meditation Center in Northern California and experience my first silent *vipassana* (insight meditation) retreat, envisioned by Dharma Teacher Marlene Jones, and many others.

As I walked through the gate for retreatants, headed toward my room, I grew humble amid the vast hills. I greeted many friends and unknown faces. Everyone looked familiar, being that the retreat was for African Americans. But that familiarity was that kind worn not only in our distinctive hair and range of brown skin tones, but also in our continuous longing to evolve beyond the suffering in our lives that we seemed to wear on our shoulders.

There would be no writing or reading, but rather an intense focus on the human condition. There, at the retreat, we were to just sit and see into the mirror of our lives.

Snug inside my sleeping bag, I missed the early morning bell. I hadn't gotten a rest among trees for some time. A wild turkey gobbled, perhaps herding young ones to a safe place. I yawned, moving slowly out of bed, even though I was late. In the bathroom, the sink was wet; the rugs near the showers were wet. Everyone but me had come and gone. I knew where I was supposed to be, but I wasn't there, and it didn't bother me. I put on a warm sweat suit after washing the sleep from my face.

Then it was time for the trek. Not a big trek; just a little trek up a small hill to the meditation hall. One foot, then the other. The trek took longer than I thought. Maybe I had better trot, but I didn't. I kept trekking up the hill, which appeared to be a mere mound covered in cement.

Finally, I opened the glass doors, found a place for my shoes in the entrance area. Everyone was seated. I walked in and bowed—just to be bowing, because I had yet to learn the meaning and power in a bow. Then I noticed the statues of Buddha and Kuan Yin on an altar at the back of the room. A sea of black folks sat quietly—a sea of darkness with swirls of brown and beige. I crossed into the sea. I was no longer alone, having joined the silence.

I shifted above my sitting cushion—left, right, left, right. I slipped off, slid back on, looked around. My body was not ready; my mind was preoccupied with who was looking. But there was no one paying any attention to me. Once I could see no one was looking, I entered the quiet sea again.

I began to think, of course.

I thought that I have always gone about life aware of the disharmony between what I observed, learned, and practiced in life. One of my earliest revelations was that freedom, joy, and love did not come to me just because I was human. Having Christian parents with black, southern Louisiana roots dictated a certain way I saw suffering; I saw it as out of reach, the way I heard warnings of caution, the way I felt God was watching. Those roots were just short of liberation. So I had been suffering greatly before the retreat, having to accept myself as I was and not wanting to accept at the same time. *Love me, love me, everyone. Everyone but me needs to love me, because I can't.* I shifted to allow the blood to flow in my legs.

My eyes were closed, and I was invisible in the black sea of silence. There was a little coughing, slow breathing, and no contact in the room. No talking. But my mind did speak, loud and clear.

"You don't belong!"

What?

"We don't like you!"

I thought so.

"We don't like you!"

Silence, I said to my mind. *Please be still.* I moved, holding my stomach, fighting tears, thinking, thinking, thinking, again, "They don't love me, my own people?"

No, I don't love me.

I opened my eyes to wipe away the tears. No one must know that I had just had a falling out with my own mind.

The bell rang to end the meditation. There was no peace yet. I looked around the room. *Where is it? Where is that peace, that calm I need?*

The black sea was still silent. I was thirsty, in the middle of this sea, but I couldn't drink it. I was thirsty enough to listen to the Dharma teachers. "Please take a deep breath," a teacher said.

I listened to the Dharma teachers share their stories, finding myself being still in the midst of my suffering, their suffering, our suffering. "Oh, it's nobody's suffering," they say. *Is that what is to be understood by their sharing?* In each of their stories, there I was. My thoughts ballooned and sagged

and ballooned again. Not a one popped. The pain of disre-
gard, the dehumanization of black people that the teachers
spoke about squeezed the walls of my heart. I searched for
my breath, finding it each time. *Ah, breathe*, I said to myself.

*Can I shout in this meditation hall? Can I yell, "Amen! You
know you're right!" like we do in church?"*

When the teachers spoke of oppression, talked about life
passing by us each moment, talked about how we shouldn't
look back, shouldn't look forward, but be just here, I said,
"Um um," under my stare. We were all going to die right
here, drown right here in this sea, I was thinking.

The only way to survive was to receive the gifts that
were being offered, the gifts that each teacher, one by one,
laid down as an offering to their fellow dharma sisters and
brothers. The altar was filled with their stories.

As day four rolled around, I had learned to sit despite the
pain in my back and knees. I walked the earth as if I had
never experienced it before, wobbling at times. I learned to
breathe quietly and sometimes fiercely. I chanted. I sought,
for the umpteeth time, calm, love and peace, as if it were all
hidden under our cushions to take home.

Finally, Aba Cecile Mchardy, a *lama* (Tibetan Buddhist
teacher and spiritual mother) who came from Jamaica to
Ghana to America to teach, was available for guidance.
Friendly Dragon was the name by which she is fondly called.
She spent the first ten minutes listening to me sob. She sat.
I sobbed. So much water in the black sea, I wanted to say.
But I couldn't say a word. She never looked away from me,
not at all afraid of my grief. Never once did she move or

twitch. I knew her. I had seen her, the teacher, the healer, in my dreams.

"After fifteen years of chanting, practicing the way, I am still suffering," I finally said.

"Really. You've been practicing for fifteen years!" she said with her voice hanging in the room. I wasn't sure if she was impressed or if she was amazed that I had been practicing and was still suffering. It didn't matter.

"Yes," I cried.

Friendly Dragon, still as can be, looked me in the eyes and said in her Jamaican British accent, "You are not your mind."

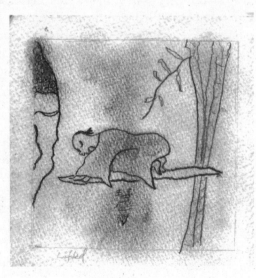

I could not understand what she was saying. My mind did not want me to think I was not it. The more her words rolled across her lips, the more the mind grabbed onto itself, to save itself and all that I perceived as life. My mind shouted, "No, you can't leave me. I have taken care of you, provided you with faith, given you intelligence, and helped you to be whatever you wanted to be. You can't think that you are not me."

I continued to listen as the teacher said, "Watch your mind, and do not attach to what it thinks. Just let it think and then watch the thoughts disappear from your mind."

She told me to ride out the delusions in my heart as if I were riding a fierce tiger. She said I would need to ride this tiger until the tiger became friendly. The tiger was not going to disappear—meaning my mind would always be there thinking. I laughed between the tears as I saw a tiger running all over the meditation hall, with me flying high above its back, but still holding on tight.

At the end of our session, I stood up, full as could be. I drank the tears down, and in the meantime, I was no longer thirsty. I walked out the guidance room holding onto the tiger and still afraid of falling into a pit of torture. But if I didn't face this fear, I would be an impostor in my life, pretending to be fearless. I wanted my mind; I wanted my dark body, the very two things that, when clung to, caused great suffering. The mind and the body are there—no need to cling to them.

By the end of the retreat, the mirror, held up by the teachings so that I could look at myself, had cracked. I could not see a whole black face, but saw one that had open spaces, a face that would allow more light in than if it were solid. Eventually, I could not see a face at all. Where and how does one live without a face?

On the last day, the sun came, but it was not the same sun as the day before or any sun of my past. The room I'd stayed in for the retreat was not the same room; the walls were not the same white. I touched the doorknob, turning it, pushing the door open then closed, understanding for the first time that I did not live behind doors, shut out from the world. Instead I lived *with* the door, experiencing its opening and closing, like my heart opened and closed.

Often I felt that I did not belong in the world, that the door to my house was the way I entered and left the world each day. Would I belong or not belong if there were no door? Is home a matter of where we enter and leave? I would carry this awakening of questions to the closing ritual.

An invitation for African Americans to sit was rare. We are more often invited to protest. When it was time to leave, one hundred African Americans and those who identified as African descent walked much more slowly than we had when we had come to the retreat. Our smiles were much gentler.

When most of the retreatants had left the grounds, I walked arm and arm with my beloved and a mutual close friend downhill, away from the meditation hall. As we slowly moved down the long road toward the parking lot, I still had tears waiting to spill down my face. The time had arrived to reenter the "real" world. It was especially time to hold myself as tenderly as I could, with the thought that being black had its gifts, but mostly I suffered from clinging to that limitation. So I vowed to practice tenderness. No more longing to be loved by others without first understanding the nature of love. This vow I had uttered more than enough times in my life, "Love thy neighbor as thyself," and now it was time to live it. "Thy neighbor" was everyone in the world, not just black people. And did I love thyself?

As the car left the center, I said farewell to the departing black sea, where they ride tigers while tears flow. There were new memories and new wisdom.

The idea that clinging to blackness as a form of empowerment could cause great suffering was difficult to digest. Zen master Huang Po taught that to make use of your mind, to think conceptually, is to leave the substance [of things] and attach yourself to form. In such a condition, we are limited to the shape and form by which we make distinctions. He goes on to say, "One Mind [a limitless open heart] is the Buddha, and there is no distinction between the Buddha and sentient things, but that sentient beings are attached to forms and so seek externally for Buddhahood." This distinction, this attachment to form, is what we experience as separation and, ultimately, as suffering.

Therefore, it was necessary for me to study clinging to the form of a dark body during zazen, not so I turn away from clinging, but so I move toward it, face it, and understand the suffering not as a reality to live by. To forget the self, in the sense of the body, is to not think of it as if it were everything there is in life. There is no tranquility in that. And yet we are constantly working to hold onto the body. We are constantly trying not to die, because our greatest fear is death.

⧉ What about death?

What is this life? What is this death? Are they not one and the same? My father, born in 1898, was sixty years old when I was born, and my mother, born in 1910, was forty-two years old. So I began to question death as a child, knowing that my parents were much older than those of the other children my age. Then a childhood friend died, and the question of death loomed over me from that time forward.

"Great is the matter of birth and death, quickly passing, passing, gone. Awake, awake, each one, awake. Don't waste this life." This is the message written on the *han*, a wooden instrument used in Japanese-styled Soto Zen centers around the world, to call practitioners to the zendo (meditation hall). So when I hear the han sounding out, I don't hesitate. I don't waste time. I stop my mental and physical activity. I listen. Then I walk to the sound of this piece of wood being tapped with a wooden mallet, sounding out, "Wake up! Life is passing, right now! Right now, you are passing." That is the most profound teaching on death I have come across in Soto Zen practice. And it is very simple to understand.

We are constantly working to hold onto the passing body. We are ever vigilant in protecting ourselves from death. Yet without a doubt, we will all drop away body and mind when we die. Even if we accomplish all that we want in life, even with the refinement of our religious and spiritual practices and our health schemes, or even if we are enlightened, we will experience death. Because we are born, we will die. And this thing called death both terrorizes and fascinates us. When I was a child, my fear of and curiosity about death were great, and as I heard death described from the church pulpit, I became intensely interested in living a spiritual life. I would go so far as to say that my ordination as a Zen priest had much to do with dedicating myself to the questions of living and dying. My ordination also may have had something to do with wanting to learn how to live life fully so that when death comes, I will be as close to my true nature as possible.

Meanwhile, I've encountered the death of loved ones and my own episodes of near death while practicing Shakyamuni Buddha's teachings. With these events, I came to see death as one of the widest gates of liberation from suffering. In death, the impermanence of all matter is revealed. I came to see that despite everything appearing the same as it was yesterday, death changed everything and everyone; it opened the mouth of the river of life, loosening our grip whether we want it to or not. I came to see that the great matter of birth and death is not great because it's scary, but because birth and death are profound in their immense capacity to arouse a loving nature, bring attentiveness to living, and, most importantly, seal an interrelationship between all that arises and ceases or all that is born and will die.

When we hear of a death, it reminds us, like nothing else in life, that we are interdependent upon one another. In death it is customary to stop and become aware of the loss of life, the loss of ourselves in relationship with other living beings. In many churches and temples around the world, bells ring out to signal a death. When the bells ring, it is time to stop and notice the continuing cycle of birth and death.

Eihei Dogen, the founder of Soto Zen, said if you see death as something over there, then you are viewing your life from outside of it. We can't look at the cycle of birth and death as objects outside of life, but must awaken to it

from within the cycle. Then we will see life as no more than dying. Life is death, and death is life.

I have become less afraid of death by seeing it as a continuum of life's moments, without beginning or end. Actual death may be the greatest healing journey of transformation that we find ourselves aspiring to while living. In such aspiration, our life becomes our death, and I imagine death becoming life. The prophet Khalil Gibran put it so well in his teaching titled "the river of silence" in *The Prophet*:

> *Then Almitra spoke, saying, We would ask now of Death.*
> *And he said:*
> *You would know the secret of death.*
> *But how shall you find it unless you seek it in the heart of life?*
> *The owl whose night-bound eyes are blind unto the day cannot unveil the mystery of light.*
> *If you would indeed behold the spirit of death, open your heart wide unto the body of life.*
> *For life and death are one, even as the river and the sea are one.*
>
> *In the depth of your hopes and desires lies your silent knowledge of the beyond;*
> *And like seeds dreaming beneath the snow your heart dreams of spring.*
> *Trust the dreams, for in them is hidden the gate to eternity.*

Your fear of death is but the trembling of the shepherd when he stands before the king whose hand is to be laid upon him in honour.

Is the shepherd not joyful beneath his trembling, that he shall wear the mark of the king?

Yet is he not more mindful of his trembling?

For what is it to die but to stand naked in the wind and to melt into the sun?

And what is it to cease breathing, but to free the breath from its restless tides, that it may rise and expand and seek God unencumbered?

Only when you drink from the river of silence shall you indeed sing.

And when you have reached the mountain top, then you shall begin to climb.

And when the earth shall claim your limbs, then shall you truly dance.

⁂ Are Buddhists seeking oneness?

In Buddha's teachings, there is a discussion of interrelationship or interbeing as the foundation for life. In the secular world, these teachings have been described as a concept of oneness. Yet the experience of interrelationship or oneness goes far beyond an idea of it.

Three days after coming back from a trip to Malaysia for the Sakyadhita ("daughters of Buddha") International

Conference on Buddhist Women in 2007, I still heard the voices of the young Tibetan nuns singing "We Shall Overcome" (derived from Charles Tindley's gospel song "I'll Overcome Some Day," 1900). The nuns sang the song as many African Americans had done during the civil rights movement in North America, long before any of the nuns were born. Yet the song emerged from deep in their hearts, testifying that they believed liberation was possible today, not someday. I listened to the song from the other side of the curtains that divided a dormitory of hundreds of lay and ordained daughters of Buddha. I sang with them, but it was a silent rendition, as I wanted to hear their sweet voices in harmony with my own heart. Tears welled up in my eyes.

That moment was oneness. It was oneness of the heart that stretched across generations, cultures, religions, biological ages, and continents. In dharma, oneness is the synchronicity of hearts, which happens whether we can physically see each other or not. In oneness, difference exists, but harmonizes with what appears to be sameness. Oneness cannot be produced, planned, or shaped. Oneness is a living spirit that resides in those of us who are open enough to experiencing it when it arrives. And when it arrives, we no longer feel alone.

For some of us, that oneness can threaten our sense of identity—an identity created over a lifetime. Can this identity exist within the spirit of oneness? Do we really know who we are? On the web site Global Oneness Project (*globalonenessproject.org*), a spiritual teacher named Adyashanti is described as saying that, "in the development of human consciousness, there comes a shift from a sense of a separate self toward the experience of unity. He points out that the fear of losing our individual identity keeps us from making this shift, and by confronting our fear we come into love." The description of his interview notes, "Adyashanti also suggests that reaching a point of crisis can allow an opportunity for consciousness to shift, individually and collectively."

The nuns and I sung a song that grew popular during a time of crisis in the United States. While protesting during the civil rights movement, many may have found themselves being a kind of people they didn't consider themselves to be. It was difficult for many church-loving black people to fight on homeland when their identity was that of peace-loving human beings. For the oneness to arise and take up residence inside them, many had to abandon some part, if not all, of their peaceful identity. Perhaps the civil rights movement wasn't so much about being black as much as it was about embracing liberation. Perhaps black people were not fighting for themselves as much as making way for the true spirit of oneness in this nation.

⅔ What about multiculturalism in Buddhist communities?

Imagine you have arrived on the path of Buddha's teachings. Your hope is that everyone you practice with is loving, caring, open, accepting of you. You want this new place of Buddha, this new family, to be better than the places you've been, the family you've had. In the new place, you assume there is harmony. All you have to do is sit down, take a deep breath, be quiet, and forget about the world, thinking a Buddhist practice will take care of everything.

Then something or someone reminds you that the world is within each and everyone one of us—that the world is inside the Buddhist center, nunnery, or monastery. You still hear speech you had hoped to not hear in your new precious environment. You see things or someone that you thought would never be at your new place. Your teacher and fellow dharma brothers and sisters irritate you in the same way as your personal family members or as strangers with a different way of living might do.

Then you realize that you haven't gotten away at all. You have not gone off to some place that is not on this planet. You're just seeing different scenery of the troubled society, with its troubled people, and it's much like that which you have lived with all your life. Suddenly, you are just as fearful or outraged as you were before you took that deep breath for the first time in meditation.

We bring our negative preferences, distortions, and notions of each other into our spiritual places to transform these negative things. As a result, these things intensify because we are praying and working on them in ritual together. Things get tight with our different ways of being and our ignorance of one another.

The seeds of Buddhist traditions in the world have largely come from mostly homogenous communal Eastern societies, where multiculturalism may or may not affect the Sangha.

Today, these traditions have made their way to many multicultural societies, including the United States, where there are great differences in beliefs and values. Therefore, within our practice of the Buddha's teachings, we are faced constantly with the practice of harmonizing these differences. In a multicultural society, at the center of our Buddhist practice, is the vow to overcome thoughts of one kind of people being superior or inferior to the other. To value all life is to vow to share the essence of each other. Harmony is not uniformity, but rather accepting the multiplicity of oneness.

Before I accepted that sitting meditation was a valid response (but not the only response) to hatred and ignorance in the world, I thought it necessary to fix things, to analyze the situation, to carry the burden of making things better for those who suffer. I did this simply because I personally had suffered through the challenges of living in a multicultural society.

Prior to planting my feet on the Buddha's path, I was angry at the universe, angry at God, as if either one were a person out there somewhere doing bad things to us. When I discovered that the anger that resided in my heart was the same as the hatred I experienced, the depth of suffering in the world became clear. I had closed my heart to people who were different than me, especially those I thought were considered better than me. I was clear that the rage within would need tending to with sweet loving care in my practice of dharma. It was clear that my journey in Sangha would be complete openness of the heart.

Any person who aspires to love and peace in a multicultural environment makes great efforts to achieve openness of the heart. Yet openness of the heart can be especially difficult if there is a sense that others' hearts are closed to you. As a young dark child, I experienced the difficulty of racial prejudice, and still today as I practice in Buddhist communities, there is a tension of feeling African and being buddha, or more specifically, a tension between difference and sameness.

In the *Sandokai*, a teaching by Chinese Ch'an master Shitou Xiqian (or known as Japanese Zen master Sekito Kisen) poetically speaks to the difficult question of how the oneness of things and the multiplicity of things coexist. He eloquently wrote, "Trunk and branches share the essence;

revered and common, each has its speech." The one trunk shares the essence of being a tree; yet the trunk has its oneness and relationship with multiple roots, and the branches are multiple while having a relationship with the one trunk. "Each has its own speech" addresses the multiplicity in the oneness creating what is called harmony.

Harmonizing the many cultures that exist in Sangha includes creating an environment for (A) practicing heartfelt speech that arouses compassion and love, (B) studying one's own store consciousness of love and hate that derives from family and ancestors, and (C) developing active, skillful, and wholesome social engagement between Sangha members, in accord with the precepts and the Eightfold Path (discussed earlier in this book).

How do we practice oneness in the presence of harmful discrimination?

In sitting meditation, this question has resided in the pit of my belly, with no words. When I began a meditation practice, it had lived there so long that the rawness it had caused could be felt when I was silent.

At first, there was a tendency to hold my stomach in and suppress the pain. There was a tendency to say it was not there or I didn't feel anything. But when I breathed deeply, there it was. And if I kept breathing, the pain lessened. So I have made a practice of breathing, sitting in a relaxed posture of alertness, feeling myself healing by just being aware, by just witnessing the mind, with no words.

And as the healing continued in each breath and after I'd been sitting for hours, days, months, and years, I can actually feel what was once only intellectualized that oneness was not one thing, but a union of *all* things within this life. And it was not a union that becomes one glob or melts away differences, but rather a union in which you can see one thing from the other. In the *Jewel Mirror Samadhi*, Ch'an master Dongshan Liangjie described this experience when he wrote, "Filling a silver bowl with snow, hiding a heron in the moonlight. Taken as similar, they're not the same; when you mix them, you know where they are." Nothing is lost.

So with understanding, we can see that the distinction in the union, the difference in the harmony, the African in the Buddha, is not distinction for the purpose of harmful discrimination or domination, but rather an experience of how multiplicity is within oneness. The separations created between humans are experienced in this country as a result of not understanding that difference is within oneness. Multiplicity is mistaken for each one, each thing, being separate, or multiplicity, often, is seen as not being within the realm of harmony.

With the condition of separation, one may think he or she can hate another without hating oneself. But it is impossible to truly love while hating. I have said that I love black people. But in sitting meditation, I have come to see that it is not *always* love that I feel, but rather some sort of favoritism or preference that I have with people that appear to be like me. I see that if I truly loved, my love would not stop at the borders of my own preferences. When I speak of preferences and discrimination, I am not dismissing our country's need to end the suffering caused by one group dominating another, by suppressing life in a group of people. I am not saying that merely with the realization of love through sitting meditation can we end a long history of oppression. If only life were that simple and one-dimensional.

Within multicultural societies, including communities of dharma practitioners, we are learning to walk the path of compassion and wisdom with personal honesty and unbound intimacy. The practice is to make companions of difference and harmony, see them both as oneness itself. We cannot take the teaching of harmony to serve the desire for sameness and comfort.

Difference within community can be experienced as difficult and messy at times. Harmony is also difficult and messy. When we take refuge in Sangha, we are dedicating ourselves to practicing Buddha's teachings of oneness *within* our inherent differences. We practice this teaching for the rest of our lives.

When I practice with the tension of feeling African and being buddha, I am settling my breath on the oneness that is filled with all of what is. I practice compassion for my being easily hurt when the wounding arises from racism and other harmful human conditions. I say this hurt is not mine, but a pain of this world; it belongs to no one and yet everyone is affected by it. In the pain, I recognize that the causes of racism, not the racists, have formed the tears on my face. I am suddenly at a crucial place of deciding what action to take. I respond to the tears first, which leads to compassion and awareness of the conditioning that has taken place over many generations. I breathe in, and I breathe out. And then I do not cry for myself, but for the suffering in the world. That is being buddha or being on Buddha's path.

𝕏 What is "being Buddha" or being on Buddha's path?

"Being buddha," in my words, is to be the teachings. To follow the teachings of Buddha is to walk on Buddha's path, but also to come to one's own revelations, as Buddha did. You may also hear the words "Buddha way" used for what I am calling the path.

It is important to say that there are few, if any, on this earth that have the capacity to completely follow all of the teachings of Buddha. Often people expect Buddhists to be loving and kind because of the teachings. However, all people are constantly faced with human conditioning in various degrees every moment. The suffering we have endured throughout our lives obstructs our actions. For this reason, we work toward mindfulness, compassion for our not being upright at all times, and wisdom to begin again and again when life is interrupted with our own blindness.

However, it is also this human conditioning that leads us to the path. We began to understand the path as one of awakening from the stupor caused by conditioning.

I pierced the bubble of a familiar conditioning once at a one-day sitting-meditation retreat. It was time for a meal in the zendo, following a service of chanting and bowing. A server came to our quadrant and successfully served the folks on one side. When he turned to serve me, he stumbled and dropped the whole bowl of cashew nuts meant for the bananas and buttermilk. I could see his frustration, but I was not sure if he saw mine. I was sitting *alone* on my side of the quadrant, in a room in which I was the only person of color among approximately seventy people. My conditioning said, "He dropped the nuts because he's scared of black people." Mind you, I did not know this person. I sat there, allowing my feelings to soar around the blackness.

Just I was about to get up and leave the meal, I heard this voice in my head that said, "How do you know he dropped the nuts because you're black? He could be afraid because you are awesome."

In my conditioning at the time, I had been thinking low of myself. I did not feel awesome in the zendo. With the new thoughts, I did not run out of the zendo. Instead, I felt into being awesome, a feeling I did not trust. In the end, the truth may have been that he was afraid of me because I was black, or that may not have been the case. But I did have the opportunity to see how conditioning by past incidents of hatred throughout my life was taking over a present moment. Although the experiences of hatred against me in life did occur, the true nature of life does not rest in a *negative* or *positive* sense of blackness.

An awakening began when I could see that the server and I were mirroring each other's shame for different reasons and for a different set of human conditions. In the silence, the human condition of us both was revealed in the simple act of dropping the nuts. For sure, the awakening would not cease until the end of our lives. Awakening is a lifetime journey.

⅗ Is there a book in Buddhism, like the Bible or Koran?

The teachings of Buddha, known as the Pali canon (teachings in Pali, an ancient language of India, which along with Sanskrit, is the mother tongue of English) are so vast (over 80,000) they could never be contained in one book. I attribute this vastness to the fact that Buddha teaches us to use life itself to discover the teachings, rather than the teachings being imposed upon us as if life were permanent and clearly defined. Therefore, one does not become Buddhist by simply following a book of laws. In fact, one cannot become Buddhist at all. We can only live Buddha's way.

Buddha's teachings are steeped in mysteries that are revealed in time. The Ch'an master Hsi-ch'ien, in his poem "Inquiry into Matching Halves," says investigating the mysteries like a sleuth, rather than living into them, is a waste of time. There have been many efforts to put contemporary words to the teachings of Buddha to help people investigate the mysteries, yet the words cannot replace the time it will take for the unknown to reveal itself.

If you are starting out on the path of Buddha's way, it is best to begin with the guidance of a teacher. Without a practice leader or teacher, the beginner could miss the depth of understanding needed to truly learn the teachings. As you can see, studying the Buddha taught goes far beyond any text. A teacher, senior dharma practitioner , or leader of a meditation retreat would be more helpful than a book in discovering your true nature. She or he can help reveal the motivations or intentions of your actions.

At the same time, there are three books that contain a great number of Buddha's teachings, which are presented in the way he delivered them in his voice, like sermons similar to the gospels of Jesus Christ. These three books are *The Connected Discourses of the Buddha: A Translation of the Samyutta Nikaya* by Bhikkhu Bodhi, *The Middle Length Discourses of the Buddha: A Translation of the Majjhima Nikaya* by Bhikkhu Ñānamoli and Bhikkhu Bodhi, and *The Long Discourses of the Buddha: A Translation of the Digha Nikaya* by Maurice Walshe. However, if you are new to Buddhism, I would first begin with the books listed under "Books to Turn to Next," at the back of this book.

⚅⚅ What does it mean to be ordained?

Everyone who is ordained has a reason for being called to such a way of life. According to Zenkei Blanche Hartman, the ordained person is at home right in the body and is living a life of vows.

In an ordination ceremony, there is confession and repentance to purify the mind, and there is the taking of many vows. Even if the ordained has already become a Buddha, he or she vows to continue the practice for life. After the ordination, one enters Buddha's path as a nun, a monk, or, in my case, a priest. In Soto Zen, convert North

American communities, the ordained are equally called *priest*, regardless of gender. The Soto Zen priest can be monastic and live in a monastery or be a householder and live in the world.

Since ordination, I have been contemplating how not to be a priest while being one. The "being one" part has to do with my letting family and friends know that I have committed myself to a spiritual life. Having my family and friends witness my ordination ceremony meant that they were a great part of my new devotion. Committing myself to a spiritual life is saying that I am committed to living life (all life is spiritual) in a conscious and awakened place. And if I

stumble, I am still committed to awakening and participating in the healing that needs to take place. I do not see my spiritual path as exclusively Soto Zen, but as a priest, I do see that Soto Zen is a major passageway through which I become awake to life *and* death.

The "not being a priest" part has to do with not being caught up with being somebody more special than others. I am as ordinary as the rain dropping on a leaf. And mind you, ordinary is beautiful. Ordinary is peaceful and restful. When I sit silently in meditation, the tears begin to fall, and that is when I am ordinary, like any other living being. There is joy when I can remember the mundane necessity of just catching my breath.

What about renunciation and austerity?

Renunciation is not a life or vow of poverty and discomfort. Swami Prabhavananda said that one spiritual teacher could live in poverty and the other in luxury, and both be steeped in spiritual ignorance. He went further to say that renunciation is the giving up of everything—unattachment to being rich, to being poor, to possessions, to no possessions. Renunciation is to cease craving things. In that sense, renunciation is an inner life that no one can see and that cannot be judged from the outside. A spiritual person is never eager to convince people of his or her spiritual nature by using renunciation as a measure of faith.

The austerity one might see in a devotee or ordained Buddhist is a practice of not being involved in everything, conserving one's energy for a single-minded practice of seeing into one's true nature. It is not cultivating scarcity for the sake of being spiritual. All of life is spiritual.

❧ Why do monks, nuns, and priests shave their heads and wear robes?

According to Sensei Zenkei Blanche Hartman, shaving the head is a symbolic action taken at ordination. The shaved head and the robe that is given symbolize that one has released the bonds of attachment of a self-centered life and has entered the compassionate path handed down by Buddha. The person has devoted his or her life to awakening, to living life as a bodhisattva. Bodhisattvas are those who see that all beings are liberated before ending their own suffering.

Shaving one's head and making a life commitment to the Sangha is the utmost act of *dana*. *Dana* is the Pali word for giving and receiving, but it literally means the relinquishment of self. It is a dying away of what used to be one's life.

❧ Can you tell me something about the altars or shrines seen in centers and homes?

Shrines or Buddhist altars are created to remind us of compassion, wisdom, peace, harmony, and forgiveness. When I see a statue of Buddha on my altar, resting in a peaceful position with his eyes closed, it reminds me to breathe and let go. I can sit at the altar without any agenda. I have been known to lie down in front of my altar and cry for no particular reason other than to sink into the earth I walk on.

In our society, there are many shrines that strengthen our memory of purpose, religious beliefs, values, and social/political history. There are also sacred shrines for the loss of lives in war or disaster. At these shrines, there can be collective healing, prayer, and meditation.

An altar or shrine, for me, would be that area of my home that would not impose an idea or vision for religious practice, but one that would assist in bringing forth compassion and wisdom.

Malidoma Somé, a spiritual teacher of the African Dagara tribe, says that when we step into a shrine (or come

before an altar), "We are invited to forget time and the mundane world so that we can focus on our deeper selves and on the timeless realities that can be seen in the natural world that surrounds us." Contrary to popular thinking, the many statues on Buddhist altars are not idols to be worshipped; instead, they are symbols that return us to the silence of nature. The statues of Buddha, bodhisattvas, and deities are reminders of the ancient teachings.. The items on an altar, such as fire from the candles, and water and food from the earth, represent the elements of nature. Incense (and/or flowers) is offered to honor Buddha at the altar. Incense is said to refresh the mind and body, bring alertness, act as a companion in solitude, and bring a sense of peace. Lighting incense has long been considered a way of purifying the environment and helping to heal those in its presence. Incense has been a part of Buddhist rituals and ceremonies for centuries.

Everything on the Buddhist altar relates to the five senses and can awaken the consciousness of those senses, so that we can clearly see our harmful attachments and attractions that cause suffering.

33 Are all Buddhists vegetarian?

In general, Buddhists aspire to avoid killing any living being, and avoid participating in the killing of living beings, by not eating meat, fish, or fowl. There are some Buddhists traditions that are strict about being vegetarians or vegan, and there are others that are not as fundamental about not eating meat, fish, or fowl (and meat byproducts such as milk, cheese, and eggs).

The point is, if you do indulge in eating flesh, then you have to ask about the effects of your actions on yourself, others, and the environment.

I resonate with the macrobiotic philosophy that food is medicine and that we are made up of what we eat. The quality of your life is shaped by your cells, your cells are shaped by food, and the food you eat shapes the environment. Therefore, it is important to establish an interrelationship with what we eat and the wellness of living beings.

🥢 Is Buddhism in Eastern countries different than Buddhism in North America?

After walking the path of Dharma for twenty-plus years, I became curious about Buddhism in the East. Also, I wanted to establish a global Sangha for myself that included more than just folks from the United States. In attending the Sakyadhita International Conference on Buddhist Women (*www.sakyadhita.org*), I have traveled to Malaysia and Mongolia and met devoted Buddhist women, lay and ordained, from over fifty countries, including Korea, Taiwan, Thailand, Sri Lanka, Mongolia, Vietnam, Australia, Germany, Sweden, India, Canada, and parts of the United States that I did not live in. Prior to these conferences, I had also been to Tamil Nadu, India.

In these travels, it was clear that the "way of being" described in Buddha's teachings runs deep into the earth of Eastern culture and customs. In those conference participants from Eastern countries, it was sometimes difficult to distinguish between the Buddha way and the everyday Eastern way of life—its ways of walking, eating, or being in community. What Buddha taught fit precisely into Eastern cosmology as it was before his enlightenment. After all, Buddha was from India. However, I imagine things in the Eastern parts of the world have changed as these places are influenced by other parts of the world. At the same time, I found that the nuns and lay Buddhist women of Malaysia and Mongolia still held to Buddhism as it was taught by Buddha, with little, if any, variation.

Is everyone welcome to the practice of chanting and sitting meditation?

You can be a beginner. You can have other spiritual or religious practices. Buddha's path is steeped in liberation from suffering. To require someone to end a spiritual path in order to take on Buddhism could bring more suffering to that person. However, if there is confusion between your various practices, it is best for you to talk it over with a teacher of the Buddhist tradition of your choice.

In America, we have many choices. It is not good to move around between traditions to gather a little from each and not stay long enough to experience the effects of one practice on your life. Pay attention to being led around by your preferences as opposed to dealing with what comes up for you in practice. At the same time, trust your instincts when it comes to your well-being. Some places of practice are multicultural; others are not. It is best to ask a friend who is already practicing to make a suggestion about where to practice. Most centers or temples do not require you to become a member. You can participate to the extent you are able. Only you can decide how far you can go and observe the effects of the path on your life as you walk.

FINAL WORDS

Understanding Buddhism is like groping in the dark. It is a mystery in which you may discover something and then you must throw it out again. Finally, when you no longer are seeking and you no longer have a fixed idea what dharma is, that very moment could be the moment in which you come to the wisdom that was planted within you long before your birth.

Know that it is difficult to learn Buddha's teachings through explanations. Know that I have made an attempt to concretize a teaching that cannot be solidified because wisdom comes from your own life. So you may still feel fuzzy about this practice. It is this fuzziness, coupled with curiosity, that has kept me on the path. I feel genuinely that Buddha intended the practice to be a continuous exploration. Once we become certain, there is no place for learning, and we find ourselves defending our idea with a partial view of things.

Maybe you know this ancient story: There was once a powerful king in India, who called all his blind retainers together to his court and then brought out one of his largest elephants before them, asking the retainers what they thought of it. Being born blind, they had never seen an elephant, but now, In obedience to the royal command, they all came around the animal. Each of them touched only a certain portion of the huge body and came to the hasty conclusion that the portion he handled was really the entirety of the beast.

Those that touched the tail thought the elephant was like a broom; those that touched the leg thought it resembled a huge column; those that touched the back imagined the elephant had a body with the shape of a gigantic drum; those that handled the ear thought it reminded them of the wing of a bird; those that touched the tusk thought it had the shape of a horn. Though none of them could describe the complete and exact figure of the elephant, each was narrow-minded enough to insist on the verity of his testimony. The king was very much amused to see how utterly they failed to comprehend the object and how fruitless their quarreling was.

Buddha not Buddha

Each had a view or an understanding of the elephant that was not the whole view. The practice of Buddha's teachings is similar in that we can only see so much of it at a time.

Because it is as unknown as the elephant was to the blind retainers, your walk on the path maybe completely ambiguous. We don't know the whole truth of the teachings, and many interpretations of Buddha's teachings exist in the world. The delivery of his teachings is dependent upon the insight and hearts of the teachers to whom the teachings were transmitted.

Buddha's teachings are not an instant formula for nirvana. Once you begin to purify your heart-mind, you can count on a dust ball of illusion blowing in so that you cannot clearly see. Suddenly, you are groping in the dark once more as blindness recurs in your life. The *Book of Serenity*, a book of ancient Zen *koans*, or spiritual questions, translated by Thomas Cleary, says in "Case One":

> The unique breeze of
> reality—
> Don't let it blow
> in your eyes;
> it's especially
> hard to get out.

The practice is to constantly clear from our minds what we think and feel to be real. We have a place in the world in which to stand upright and share the gift of insight we were all born with. We could spend our time being afraid of what others think or wait for another's opinion of our lives, but eventually the suffering will bellow so loud we will need to quiet it. At least this was the case for me when I entered the Buddha way.

We live in times that are different from Buddha's time. But the one thing that remains a common ground for all living beings is honoring our precious lives.

Here are some things I thought would be helpful for integrating the messages in this book:

First, begin a letting go process. Let go of the words here. Get out of your head and try not to compare Buddha's teachings to other ones or analyze the problems that surface for you based on what is written. Allow any new discoveries about yourself to arise. Allow time and space (rather than your intellect) to bring together what teachings are needed in your life.

Second, we all live busy lives, but if you take five or ten minutes a day to stop and be alone in silence, you will find some ease in the day. This ease will lead to patience. All spiritual paths require a great amount of patience.

Third, have conversations with others about what you have read in this book. Sharing your visions for a spiritual life gives friends and family a chance to support you, as well as gain a respect for the things you find along the path of life. Even if you find others reacting negatively to your explorations, see how committed you are to your life's vision or explore your own spiritual motivations as a process of understanding the challenges. Talk with a teacher or senior practitioner on the path.

Fourth, continue to live life as an inquiry. Although I have answered some questions, there are many more questions to be asked and a longer conversation to be had about Buddha's teachings.

I hope this book has helped you. Even if this path is not for you, I hope you could find something to help heal and transform the suffering in your life.

May you find peace with the uncertainty of life. And may the merit of these words go forth into the world for the benefit of all and to help ease our collective suffering. May we heal to the fullest extent possible.

In peace, in joy, in wellness.

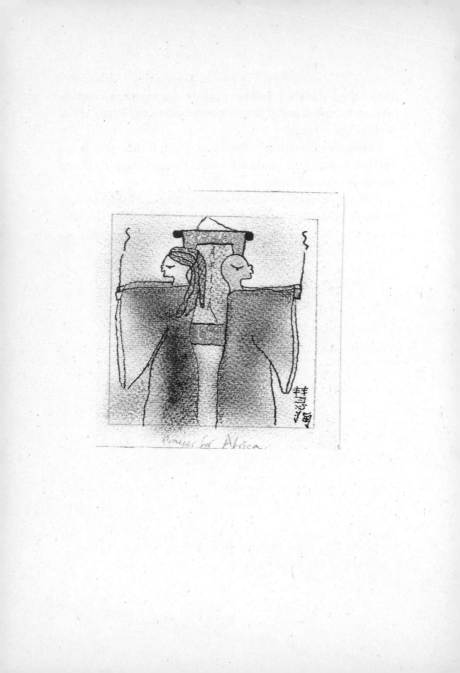

Prayers for Africa

RESOURCES TO TURN TO NEXT

Books

BEGINNING BUDDHISM

Chödrön, Pema. *Start Where You Are: A Guide for Compassionate Living*. Boston: Shambhala, 2004.

Chödrön, Thubten. *Buddhism for Beginners*. Ithaca, NY: Snow Lion Publications, 2001.

Farrer-Halls, Gill. *The Illustrated Encyclopedia of Buddhist Wisdom*. Wheaton, IL: Quest Books, 2000.

Hanh, Thich Nhat. *Heart of the Buddha's Teachings*. New York: Three Rivers Press, 1999.

Khema, Ayya. *Being Nobody, Going Nowhere*. Boston: Wisdom Publications, 1987.

Kornfield, Jack. *The Path of Heart*. New York: Bantam, 1993.

Suzuki, Shunryu, with David Chadwick. *Beginner's Mind, Zen Mind*. 40th anniversary edition. Boston: Shambhala, 2010.

Suzuki, Shunryu. *Not Always So: Practicing the True Spirit of Zen*. Reprint edition. New York: HarperOne, 2008.

Adielé, Faith. *Meeting Faith: The Forest Journals of a Black Buddhist Nun*. New York: W.W. Norton, 2005.

Baldoquín, Hilda Ryumon Guitiérrez, ed. *Dharma, Color, Culture: New Voices in Western Buddhism*. Berkeley, CA: Parallax Press, 2004.

Gross, Rita. *Buddhism After Patriarchy: A Feminist History, Analysis and Reconstruction of Buddhism*. Albany, NY: SUNY Press, 1992.

Murcott, Susan. *The First Buddhist Women: Poems and Stories of Awakening, Second edition*. Berkeley, CA: Parallax, 2006.

Sam, Canyon. *Sky Train: Tibetan Women On the Edge of History*. Seattle: University of Washington Press, 2009

Schireson, Grace, and Miriam Levering. *Zen Women: Beyond Tea Ladies, Iron Maidens, and Macho Masters*. Boston: Wisdom Publications, 2009.

Teasdale, Sallie. *Women of the Way: Discovering 2,500 Years of Buddhist Wisdom*. New York: HarperOne, 2006.

Willis, Jan. *Dreaming Me: Black, Baptist, and Buddhist—One Woman's Spiritual Journey*. Boston: Wisdom Publications, 2008.

Chödrön, Pema. *Start Where You Are: A Guide for Compassionate Living*. Boston: Shambhala Library, 2004

Chödrön, Pema. *When Things Fall Apart: Heart Advice for Difficult Times*. Boston: Shambhala, 2002.

Cleary, Thomas, trans. *Book of Serenity: One Hundred Zen Dialogues*. Boston: Shambhala, 2005.

Ferguson, Gaylon. *Natural Wakefulness: Discovering the Wisdom We Were Born With*. Boston: Shambhala, 2010.

Hanh, Thich Nhat, ed. *Together We Are One*. Berkeley, CA: Parallax, 2010.

Hanh, Thich Nhat, *Present Moment, Wonderful Moment: Mindfulness Verses for Daily Living*, 2nd edition, Berkeley CA: Parallax Press, 2006

Johnson, Charles. *Turning the Wheel: Essays on Buddhism and Writing*. New York: Scribner, 2007.

Katagiri, Dainin. *Returning to Silence*. Boston: Shambhala, 1988.

Kornfield, Jack. *The Path with Heart: A Guide Through the Perils and Promises of Spiritual Life. (1st Edition)* New York: Bantam, 1993.

Nepo, Mark. *The Book of Awakening: Having the Life You Want by Being Present to the Life You Have*. San Francisco: Conari, 2000.

Salzberg, Sharon. *Faith: Trusting Your Own Deepest Experience*. New York: Riverhead Trade, 2003.

———. *Lovingkindness: The Revolutionary Art of Happiness*. Boston: Shambhala, 1997.

Somé, Malidoma Patrice. *The Healing Wisdom of Africa*. New York: Tarcher 1999.

Suzuki, Shunryu, Edward Espe Brown, and San Francisco Zen Center. *Not Always So: Practicing the True Spirit of Zen. Reprint edition*. New York: HarperOne, 2008

Williams, Angel Kyodo. *Being Black: Zen and the Art of Living with Fearlessness and Grace*. New York: Penguin, 2002.

ADVANCED STUDY

Bodhi, Bhikkhu. *The Connected Discourses of the Buddha: A Translation of the Samyutta Nikaya*. Boston: Wisdom Publications, 2003.

Dogen, Eihei and Kazuaki Tanahashi. *Treasury of the True Dharma Eye*, Boston: Shambhala, 2011

Ñānamoli, Bhikkhu, and Bhikkhu Bodhi. *The Middle Length Discourses of the Buddha: A Translation of the Majjhima Nikaya*. Boston: Wisdom Publications, 1995.

Walshe, Maurice. *The Long Discourses of the Buddha: A Translation of the Digha Nikaya*. Boston: Wisdom Publication, 1995.

Hartranft, Chip, trans. *Yoga Sutras of Patanjali*. Boston: Shambhala Classic, 2003.

Audiobooks

Beck, Charlotte Joko. *Living Everyday Zen*. Boulder, CO: Sounds True, 2008.

Chödrön, Pema. *How to Meditate*. Boulder, CO: Sounds True, 2007.

Hanh, Thich Nhat. *The Present Moment*. Boulder, CO: Sounds True, 2003.

———. *Touching the Earth*. Boulder, CO: Sounds True, 2004.

Kornfield, Jack. *After the Ecstasy, the Laundry*. Boulder, CO: Sounds True, 2005.

Ray, Reginald. *Meditating with the Body*. Boulder, CO: Sounds True, 2003.

Films

Grubin, David. *The Buddha: The Story of Siddhartha*. 2010.

The Four Noble Truths: His Holiness the XIV Dalai Lama (a recording of an event). 1996.

Peace Is Every Step Meditation in Action: The Life and Work of Thich Nhat Hanh. 1998.

Ray, Rick. *Ten Questions for the Dalai Lama*. 2006.

Chanting

POETIC OFFERINGS BY ZENJU EARTHLYN MANUEL

When It Rains

I fall like rain.
Some folks protect themselves from me.
Some get wet.
Zen is rain when I fall from the sky.
And now I have arrived.
It's muddy and I can't stand it.
But only for a moment;
I stay muddy.
Zen is muddy.
Wet, because . . .
Just because . . .

At some moment in the future,
I will dry in the sun and rise towards it.
Zen is sunny,
Until it is time again to fall like rain.

But there really aren't any words for this
rising and falling.
If I had time I would simply roll in the grass
Like when I was five years old,
rolling on my father's St. Augustine grass,
Neighbors laughing, eating, on the front porch with
Mom and Dad;
my sisters rolling, rolling in the grass with me.
Our play clothes stained green forever.

That's me.
No, not the little girl;
the green stain!
Don't worry it will fade, slowly,
until there is nothing.
No Me.
No Zen.

For All Beings

May all beings be cared for and loved,
Be listened to, understood and acknowledged despite
different views,
Be accepted for who they are in this moment,
Be afforded patience,
Be allowed to live without fear of having their lives
taken away or their bodies violated.
May all beings,

Be well in its broadest sense,
Be fed,
Be clothed,
Be treated as if their life is precious,
Be held in the eyes of each other as family.
May all beings,
Be appreciated,
Feel welcomed anywhere on the planet,
Be freed from acts of hatred and desperation including
war, poverty, slavery, and street crimes,
Live on the planet, housed and protected from harm,
Be given what is needed to live fully, without scarcity,
Enjoy life, living without fear of one another,
Be able to speak freely in a voice and mind of undeni-
able love.
May all beings,
Receive and share the gifts of life,
Be given time to rest, be still, and experience silence.
May all beings,
Be awake.

Endless Wells

In the desert of life,
We long for ourselves,
missing the dark watery caves we came from,
We long for that water, again and again,
Until finally the teacher comes along and reminds us
how to drink from our own endless wells.

ACKNOWLEDGMENTS

I honor all of those who have taught me along the way. I especially thank those who have supported my walk with these teachings: Diana Carrington, Zenkei Blanche Hartman, Shosan Victoria Austin, Teah Strozer, Kiku Christina Lehnherr, the late Mitsuzen Lou Hartman, and Ryumon [Hilda] Gutiérrez Baldoquín who gave me the dharma name *Ekai Zenju* ("Ocean of Wisdom," "Complete Tenderness"). I would also like to thank Hozan Alan Senauke, for taking time to read and make comments on the manuscript. Finally, I would like to express my deep gratitude to my sisters, Lawrencetta Manuel and Suesette Manuel, and to Simbwala Schultz, for her love and endurance.

ABOUT THE AUTHOR

PHOTO: *Simbwala Schultz*

Rev. Zenju Earthlyn Marselean Manuel, Ph.D., has practiced Buddha's teachings for more than twenty years, initially entered Nichiren Buddhism (Soka Gakkai International) in 1988 and in 2003 entered into the Soto Zen tradition. She was ordained as a priest in 2008 by S Zenkei Blanche Hartman at the San Francisco Zen Center. Zenju is a contributing author to *Together We Are One*, edited by Thich Nhat Hanh; *Dharma, Color, and Culture: New Voices in Western Buddhism,* edited by Hilda Ryumon Gutiérrez Baldoquín; and authored many articles in *Turning Wheel* Magazine of the Buddhist Peace Fellowship. She also contributed "What Unknowing Things Know: The Zen Liberation in the Art of Romare Bearden" in the *International Review of African American Art* special issue on Eastern influences on African American art. For more information, visit her website, *www.zenjuearthlynmanuel.com*.

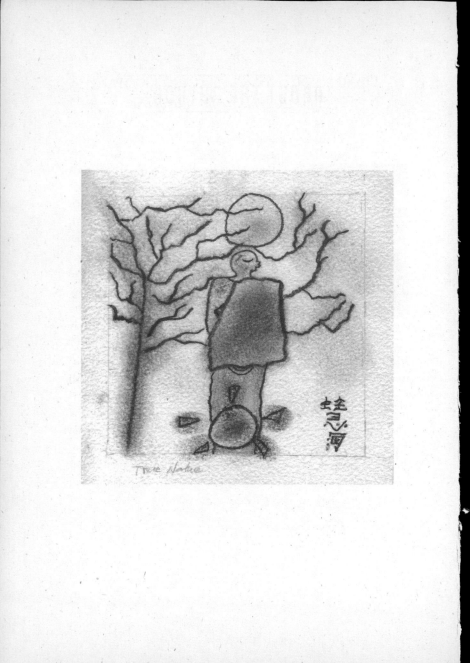

True Nature